Really Care for Them

PRAISE FOR
REALLY CARE FOR THEM

"*Really Care For Them* provides a message that will do more than enhance your performance, it will enhance your life: ABC–Always Be Caring!"

—**Hendrie Weisinger**, Ph.D., *New York Times* Best-Selling Author of *Performing Under Pressure* and *The Unlikely Art of Parental Pressure*

"Read, understand, and reflect on the wisdom in this book and watch your sales grow exponentially! *Really Care For Them* is rocket fuel for your sales organization. Every VP of Sales should buy this book for each person on their team. Mareo McCracken delivers an artful method for providing sustainable success in selling."

—**Skip Prichard**, CEO, OCLC, Inc., *Wall Street Journal* Best-Selling Author of *The Book of Mistakes: 9 Secrets to Creating a Successful Future*

"Mareo McCracken does the seemingly impossible by codifying the intangibles that make good salespeople great: Building relationships, listening thoughtfully, responding with emotional intelligence and empathy – and most importantly, doing so in an authentic, genuine, and unforced way. *Really Care For Them* is the definitive sales playbook."

—**Jeff Haden**, Inc. Columnist, Author of *The Motivation Myth*

"*Really Care For Them* is accessible, authentic, heartfelt, and wise, all at the same time. It does what you wish all books would do: it doesn't shout at you or lecture you, it takes your hand and guides you, one little jewel of insight at a time. I don't just like Mareo's book, I love it."

—**John David Mann**, Coauthor of *The Go-Giver*, *Out of the Maze*, and *The Latte Factor*

"In *Really Care For Them*, Mareo McCracken gets to the heart of what it TRULY takes to sell and succeed. The secrets of what separates top performers, from average performers, and what drives those who always do what it takes. This is a must-read for anyone looking to take their career and their life to the next level. Mareo's gift with stories, strategies and the ability to structure chapters so the learning is deepened and your return on investment is maximized."

—**Meridith Elliott Powell**, Business Growth Strategist, Award-Winning Author of *THRIVE: Turning Uncertainty to Competitive Advantage.*

"What gets the best sellers out of bed in the morning isn't an opportunity to take down big deals, negotiate lucrative contracts or cash commission checks. It's the opportunity to help customers they know are struggling to do it better. And, as Mareo argues in this book, when they focus on that outcome, the other stuff takes care of itself."

—**Matt Dixon**, Coauthor of *The Challenger Sale* & *The Challenger Customer*

"Close your eyes, crack open this book, and randomly point at something on the page you've turned to. It's pure gold. Every little bit in this book will inspire and fortify you in sales (and in all you do!). I recommend taking it in small bites and savoring every quote, story, and nugget in this one!"

—**Deb Calvert**, Coauthor of *Stop Selling & Start Leading*

"For years, Mareo McCracken has been a gift, caring for and delivering huge value to the sales community. In this fantastic new book, *Really Care for Them*, Mareo delivers again and shows us why and how the best sales-people care the most—about their profession and their customers. If you want to up your sales game, increase your 'care game' and the results will follow."

—**Mike Weinberg**, Author of *New Sales. Simplified.* & *Sales Management. Simplified.*

"Mareo is the ultimate student of the great game of sales. He's read every-thing, knows everyone, and has synthesized the best practices for those who sell from a place of service and contribution. Pick up a copy of *Really Care for Them* and sell more—and feel good about how you do it."

—**Anthony Iannarino**, Author of *The Only Sales Guide You Will Ever Need*, *The Lost Art of Closing*, and *Eat Their Lunch*

"Mareo's book revolves around one simple truth, you can't care for anyone else (e.g., your customers) unless you begin to care about yourself as a sales professional first. If there is something missing in your sales growth, this book will help you figure out what you need to do. If you're in sales, I highly recommend *Really Care For Them*!"

—**Victor Antonio**, Founder of the Sales Velocity Academy, YouTube's #1 Most Popular Sales Trainer & Author of *Sales Ex-Machina*

"It's time for the customer to be the center of the sales process and this book does just that. Too many salespeople have over-complicated things and in so doing made the customer an after-thought or worse yet, a victim of the sales process. In this powerful book, *Really Care For Them*, you'll see how to make the customer the hero they should be and by doing so you will come to love sales for what it is, people helping people."

—**Mark Hunter** "The Sales Hunter" Author of *A Mind for Sales* and *High-Profit Prospecting*

"McCracken has cracked the sales code in his new book, *Really Care For Them*. Through his focus on putting the proper care into the sales process by focusing on meeting the unique needs of customers, he highlights that everyone sells, but that no one does it well unless they care more. I recommend this book for anyone wanting to be the master in their own sales domain."

—**Heather R. Younger**, Best-Selling Author of *The 7 Intuitive Laws of Employee Loyalty* and *The Art of Caring Leadership*

"Salespeople often communicate with prospects in ways that tell prospects the meeting purpose is to get a commission check. Not only does this book raise awareness of this issue, but it also teaches you how to communicate in a meaningful way with prospects to create trusting relationships. This shift in communication differentiates you from the masses of salespeople calling on this prospect. And trust is one of the keys to win more deals at the prices you want! Every salesperson should read this book!"

—**Lee Salz**, Best-Selling Author of *Sales Differentiation*

"In the world of modern selling, developing a strong sense of authenticity and conviction in your ability to help your customers is key to growing your business. Customers can tell if you care or not! *Really Care For Them* is full of actionable insights that salespeople of all experience levels can use to do both."

—**David Priemer**, Founder & Chief Sales Scientist,
Cerebral Selling—Author of *Sell the Way You Buy*

"I loved every minute of unpacking what Mareo shared in his new book, *Really Care For Them*! Both the title and the literal care that he took to craft his chapters into easy-to-digest powerful nuggets of information make this the perfect 'how-to' book for someone beginning a career in sales and also sales veterans alike. I should also point out that it's a fast, fun read. With an array of books out there, it's important to point out that Mareo is 100% giving quality over quantity with this one: short chapters with valuable learnings that you will carry with you forever once you read it. It's packed to the hilt with important tips and tricks to help you learn how to truly care about Sales and rock at your job! This is a must-read for anyone that wants to learn about Sales from a place of genuine care. This book needed to be written and I can't recommend it enough to you."

—**Sangram Vajre**, Chief Evangelist and Co-Founder of Terminus and
Author of *ABM is B2B* and *Account-Based Marketing for Dummies*

"*Really Care For Them* is a book that helps everyone get on the SAME SIDE with bite-sized lessons that every seller should embrace, and every leader should reinforce with their team."

—**Ian Altman**, Founder and Coauthor of *Same Side Selling*

"*Really Care For Them* focuses on a fundamental attribute of the best salespeople. A mindset and approach that is often the differentiating factor in both simple and complex buying-cycles. Simply care more than anyone else. In a world of increasing automation, Mareo brings salespeople back to core values and reminds us that the transference of belief is a human-to-human trait, and one that can be developed and harnessed to better serve our customers."

—**Lee Bartlett**, Author of *The No.1 Bestseller*

"In true caring style, Mareo has curated for us an outstanding collection of all the best bits from books, TED talks, and podcasts on leadership, sales, communication, relationships, emotional intelligence, and soft skills, designed to not only teach us to be better salespeople, but also to become better humans. This is the first book every sales professional should read."

—**Amy Blaschka**, Forbes Columnist, Social Media Ghostwriter, and Author of *I Am*

"Mareo shows us how to use a care-based, holistic sales approach that gets results. *Really Care For Them* will help you move from salesperson to trusted value provider."

—**Richie Norton**, Best-Selling Author of *The Power of Starting Something Stupid*

"Who Cares? Everyone and in sales it matters if you care. That is the poignant message that Mareo brings to his readers in this compelling work on the humanity of selling. In this competitive world when what you sell is not that unique, how you sell matters more than anything else. If you lead by showing you care, the doors will open and you will have many more opportunities than if you do what you have always done and lead with your product or even your results. Top performers today, care. Their customers know they care and because of this they get more business and referrals to new business that keeps them performing at the top. Do you care? Read this book and find out."

—**Alice Heiman**, Founder and Chief Sales Energizer Alice Heiman, Inc.

"Sales is all about the art of the help. You must truly care about serving your most precious asset, your clients. In *Really Care For Them*, Mareo McCracken provides a masterful blueprint around care. To sell more, we must care more, and Mareo captures what sales is all about by creating a foundational roadmap for everyone in sales to lead their lives by."

—**Larry Levine**, Author of *Selling from the Heart: How Your Authentic Self Sells You*

"Mareo McCracken has masterfully explained exactly how to create the personal, empathetic, caring connection with clients that is essential to build clients for life. Read *Really Care For Them* and thrive."

—**Andrew Sobel**, Best-Selling Author of *Power Questions* and *It Starts with Clients*

"I am a Mareo fan. Period. What I love about his book, *Really Care For Them* is that he has created a literary album of simple, yet profound, insights into what is missing in so many sales scenarios, today. He cuts to the heart of what is needed in business, especially as we move deeper into this Connection Economy. I highly recommend and encourage any sales enthusiast to read his latest work!"

—**Bernadette McClelland**, CEO 3 Red Folders Academy

"In *Really Care For Them*, Mareo strips what it takes to be a high performing sales professional to its essence. There are no superfluous words, diagrams, stories. It is the essence of what it takes to sell and create value with your customers. It is the essence of the work and mindsets critical to success."

—**David Brock**, Author of *Sales Manager Survival Guide*

"*Really Care for Them*, is completely oozing with practical and timeless tips from the greatest minds in selling and personal achievement all distilled into fast-paced, easily digestible morsels by Mareo McCracken who is also one of the great minds in selling and personal achievement. For time-in to value-out you won't find a more valuable book anywhere. Every sales professional young or old regardless of industry will love and benefit from this book."

—**James Muir**, CEO of Best Practice International and Best-Selling Author of *The Perfect Close*

"It is an irony of our digital, mechanized age that caring matters now more than ever. Machines don't care, which is why caring humans will always matter. Think of *Really Care For Them* as the salesperson's field guide to caring."

—**Jim Ferrell**, Best-Selling Author and Founder of Withiii Leadership Center

"Oh, how I wish I had a chance to read *Really Care for Them* earlier in my career! This is a treasure trove! Cultivated from a lifetime commitment to learning and his own wealth of experience, Mareo has culled the best of the best sales tips and strategies, that not only demystify what it takes to succeed, but remind us who we want to be in the process."

—**Kimberly Davis**, Author of *Brave Leadership*
and Founder of OnStage Leadership

"Such an inspiring book on selling—it's about how you sell and how much you care. Mareo McCracken shows in an impressive way why selling is a journey of self-mastery."

—**Tamara Schenk**, Managing Partner at
Bartlett Schenk & Company

"Mareo McCracken has taken the most important truth behind the sales profession and delivered a book that is game-changing. It is impactful, easy to understand, and has practical application in the real world. If you are committed to improving sales results, *Really Care For Them* is a must read book."

—**Tony Hughes**, Co-Founder Sales IQ Global
Author of *The Joshua Principle* & *Combo Prospecting*
and Coauthor of *Tech-Powered Sales*

"Finally, a book that concentrates on the most important characteristic of a sales champion – YOU. Rather than load a book with sales scripts, Mareo goes beyond teaching core selling competencies and what you need to DO to succeed as a salesperson. *Really Care For Them* focuses on WHO you are, and how to make CARE your dominant customer acquisition and retention strategy. Since you can't automate relationships, *Really Care For Them* will teach you how to develop the deeper, trusting and more meaningful relationships that will help you and your customers thrive in today's environment."

—**Keith Rosen**, CEO of Profit Builders, Author of *Coaching Salespeople Into Sales Champions* and *SALES LEADERSHIP*

"As someone who's always hated the task of trying to sell, I found Mareo McCracken's philosophy a breath of fresh air: Don't focus on selling. Focus on helping others solve problems, and the sales will follow. *Really Care For Them* is packed full of useful tips for those who want to sell by putting the needs of their customer first."

—**Justin Bariso**, Inc. Columnist and Author of *EQ Applied*

"*Really Care For Them*, is an amazing collection of wisdom from so many sales and marketing thought leaders. I also like that it pushes for a formula of CARE + METHOD + VALUES + MINDSET + WORK HARD = IMPACT. Care is a key word in Mareo's book. Customers trust you when they feel that you genuinely care about their successes. Business is very much based on trust. I have even let go of salespeople that couldn't CARE about the customers' successes more than them reaching quota. Care more and apply what you learn in this book and you will sell more."

—**Christopher Engman**, Author of *Megadeals*
Founder of, and investor in twenty companies

"Mareo McCracken's passion for getting things right with the customer is certainly well-known by his many followers, followers he has rewarded with an ongoing sharing of reading recommendations for contemporary sales professionals. But in his new book, *Really Care For Them*, Mareo provides the reader with the ultimate reward: an opportunity for self-assessment and learning about the importance of trust, credibility and authenticity in sales, perhaps never more critical than in these challenging times."

—**Steve Andersen**, Author of *Beyond the Sales Process*, President and Founder, Performance Methods, Inc.

"Cows won't milk themselves." What in the heck does that mean? Read Mareo McCracken's new book, *Really Care For Them*. Written for salespeople—taking them from where they are now, to where they want to be. It's real. It's raw. It's not fluffy. It's different, easy to read, and memorable. Caring for our clients and helping them make smart decisions has been lost in the world of endless pitches. Read *Really Care for Them* and sell the right way, the easy way, the new way."

—**Joanne Black**, Author and Founder of *No More Cold Calling*

"Great sales professionals know a lot a lot about a lot. The best understand that the foundation of their success exists entirely in their ability to demonstrate true empathy. Mareo delivers a stark and poignant reminder of exactly what is required to consistently achieve sales excellence."

—**Phil M. Jones**, Author of *Exactly What to Say*

"The best sales advice I ever heard was from Zig Ziglar who advised salespeople to not think of themselves as salespeople, but instead, think of themselves as the assistant buyer. Mareo McCracken's new book will help you care enough about your customer to be the assistant buyer. *Really Care For Them* is 99 pieces of bite-sized sales wisdom no salesperson should be without."

—**Paul Smith**, Best-Selling Author of *Sell with a Story*

"Mareo has done an excellent job of compiling best practices in this practical guide: *Really Care For Them*. Account managers, customer success professionals and sales executives alike will benefit from his wisdom and advice."

—**Julie Thomas**, President & CEO of Value Selling Associates

NO ONE
REALLY
CARES ABOUT YOU, THEY ONLY
CARE
ABOUT WHAT YOU DO
FOR
THEM

How Everyone Can Use the
Power of Caring to Earn More Trust,
Grow Sales, and Increase income

NO MATTER WHAT YOU SELL
OR WHO YOU SELL IT TO

· ·

MAREO McCRACKEN

NEW YORK

LONDON • NASHVILLE • MELBOURNE • VANCOUVER

REALLY CARE FOR THEM

How Everyone Can Use the Power of Caring to Earn Trust, Grow Sales, and Increase Income, No Matter What You Sell or Who You Sell It To

Published in New York, New York, by Morgan James Publishing. Morgan James is a trademark of Morgan James, LLC. www.MorganJamesPublishing.com

Morgan James BOGO™

A **FREE** ebook edition is available for you or a friend with the purchase of this print book.

CLEARLY SIGN YOUR NAME ABOVE

Instructions to claim your free ebook edition:
1. Visit MorganJamesBOGO.com
2. Sign your name CLEARLY in the space above
3. Complete the form and submit a photo of this entire page
4. You or your friend can download the ebook to your preferred device

ISBN 9781631955778 paperback
ISBN 9781631955785 ebook
Library of Congress Control Number: 2021935179

Cover Design by:
Rachel Lopez
www.r2cdesign.com

Interior Design by:
Nickolas Crawford

Morgan James PUBLISHING

Builds

with...

Habitat for Humanity®
Peninsula and Greater Williamsburg

Morgan James is a proud partner of Habitat for Humanity Peninsula and Greater Williamsburg. Partners in building since 2006.

Get involved today! Visit
MorganJamesPublishing.com/giving-back

Really Care For Them is dedicated to the one who made this all possible, to the one who supported and encouraged and endured, to the one who cares the most, to the one who is the fuel for our happiness – to my Eternal Partner, my Answer, my Love, my Emilie. *(Plus, the title was Milie's idea!)*

This book, while for everyone who sells anything ever, is mostly for my children – Luci, Cobi, Martin, and Julia – may your life be filled with love, service, learning, connection, and adventure. You are my inspiration.

TABLE OF CONTENTS

There is an immutable truth about sales and selling: **Relationships Matter**

The hard cold fact – not opinion, scientific fact - is that humans feel first, then think. Therefore, how we feel about a person who is trying to sell us something exerts a massive, compulsory influence on our buying behavior.

Sales professionals who understand and embrace this fact are more successful by wide margins. They get that it is how they sell, not what they sell that gives them a distinct competitive advantage.

Sadly, many of today's sales "experts" and "gurus" are quick to tell you relationships don't matter in modern sales. Their endless pontification is the worst sort of pandering to salespeople who'd rather ignore the truth and take the easy way out, eschewing relationships and treating buyers like transactions. Yet, (another truth) if you treat your buyer like a transaction, they'll treat you like a transaction.

In *Really Care For Them* Mareo McCracken breaks from this dangerous narrative and gets back to the basics of what really matters in sales. In this inspirational and impactful guide, with practical tools and useful knowledge, Mareo took the most important truths in the sales profession and delivered a reference that is easy to understand, and even easier to apply.

Buyers expect more from their interactions with salespeople than a scripted pitch and regurgitated insight. They want to work with salespeople who care enough to listen, truly understand them, and craft personalized and relevant solutions. Buyers lean into this. You know this and I know this because we too are human, and we too are more likely to do business with someone who we believe cares.

The insights in this book will help you escape adversarial, competitive, self-destructive sales behaviors and instead develop a collaborative approach to selling that builds value, trust, lasting relationships, and demonstrates to your customers that you really care.

—JEB BLOUNT, CEO OF SALES GRAVY & AUTHOR OF *SALES EQ, INKED, & FANATICAL PROSPECTING*

INTRODUCTION

"Everything can be taken from a man but one thing: the last of the human freedoms—to **choose one's attitude** in any given set of circumstances, to choose one's own way."

- VIKTOR FRANKL

We all have motivators. Growing up, my entire life before the age of 18 below the poverty line was a serious motivator for me. My wonderful mother always found a way to provide. The daily choice always seemed to be between what was needed vs. what was wanted. As I got older, my ultimate focus was to help others and make sure that I never had to make that choice again.

While my experiences and the people in my life shaped me, it was my choices that had the greatest impact on my life. It is the same for you as well.

Think about this story:

In the late 1800s, there was a traveling book salesman and philosopher named McAfee. One hot summer he was trying to sell books and give talks in western North Carolina. No one was buying. Then McAfee happened upon a little 100-acre farm where he met Joseph, a farmer.

This farmer was one of 14 kids, and he ultimately had 13 children himself! Eventually, Joseph purchased two books penned by "famous" ancient philosophers. He already was more literate than anyone around, and now he became an avid reader. He loved those books and those philosophers. He loved them so much he named his next two sons after them – one son was named Cicero and another Virgil.

Cicero ended up loving reading even more than his father had. He also was the only one of the 13 children to get a college education. He was often called "lazy" because he read so much. First, he became a dentist and then went back to school to become a medical doctor.

Cicero went by his middle name, McAfee, named in honor of the salesman who sold his father the books. Cicero's 11 children became school district superintendents, colonels, doctors, dentists, and lawyers.

Think about the power of sales...
Think about the power of books...
Think about the power of reading...
Think about the power of someone doing their job...

I am thankful my great-great-grandfather listened to a traveling salesman that day. I am proud to be in sales today.

Back in North Carolina, while chopping wood at about age 70, Joseph had a severe accident. His son, Cicero, the doctor, was able to operate. He amputated the hand, stopped the bleeding, and saved his father's life. Joseph lived another 15 years. His education and love for learning was manifested in his children. Cicero's education was put to good use. I didn't learn this story until after I had been a sales professional for over 10 years. It is now my story. What we learn is only as important as what we do with our knowledge. If we learn and never share, did we really learn? If we study and never teach, are we valuable? Every person has goodness to share and experience to help mentor others.

If you don't have other options, you make do. Growing up we made do, a lot. My incredible and resilient single mother raised us six kids by working multiple jobs and instilling in us a "Get it Done!" attitude. It didn't matter what it was; if it was to be done, she did it or "helped" us do it. We learned to take the same approach. The question of how was never raised. We were expected to figure it out.

We worked a lot as a family. My mom had us do chores daily, not just on Saturdays. Weekends were even more brutal. Just ask my only two friends. They never came over until at least noon, just so they could be spared the experience. (Maybe I should have had better friends?) Getting a job outside the home at age 11 cleaning horse stalls at a local boarding stable was a relief, and so much easier than working at home. The same with mowing lawns, bagging groceries, babysitting, moving irrigation pipes, flipping burgers, shoveling snow, milking cows, and whatever else I did. Even now, I look back and can't think of any work that I have done that was more difficult than those "chores." Besides working hard, we learned to work smart (and creatively) in order to get everything done. Constraints help us succeed.

Professionally, every mistake I have ever made can be boiled down to two main reasons: I didn't know enough or I didn't care enough.

It is the same in life, leadership, and sales. Leading the entire company in sales one month to landing in the lower half the next? What happened? Did I change? What did I do wrong?

Once you get on a roll, you think you have finally learned something, finally mastered something. Then everything changes. I bet you are like me, where at first you are confused, maybe even in denial.

When I was in my first sales position out of college, we had a ranking system. It was in the days of the NCAA American College Football BCS ranking system, so obviously we called our ranking list the BCS. Every night it was updated. Every. Single. Night. That meant the entire sales team would gather to "discuss" the results. Probably not the best environment for showing customer love...

When your name begins to fall, you first ignore it, then you create excuses, and then you worry.

It is the same in any life endeavor; often we ignore and deny rather than be proactive the minute we see what is happening. It takes a minute to understand. But then you wake up, you realize, and it hurts to admit the truth. But when you ask yourself the hard questions, admitting the truth is the only way forward.

So after asking myself, I asked my early career mentors what was happening, why was I not producing? I began reading more books, I began listening to more audio programs.

When I began to ask and study, I truly began to learn. I had to admit that while maybe my "actions" hadn't changed that much, my mind was not as proactively engaged in the goal of progress. I had stopped caring.

When I first started in sales management, I messed up often. I thought the reason I was promoted was that I was good enough. In reality, I had the potential to be good enough, and that potential is what the bosses saw, yet I was nowhere near where I should have been.

I had great coaches and mentors, and eventually, I learned to manage and lead from those around me. One of my mentors came to me and asked, "We have been seeing some great growth the past few weeks. What can we attribute that to?" I provided some canned answer about being more proactive. Then he said, "Oh, you haven't been writing down what you guys are doing differently now? So, where are you on your first-offer close ratios? How are your performance reviews coming?" I didn't have a single answer.

I wasn't doing any of it. And I didn't apply my new experiences with a long-term perspective. That is when I knew I needed to change.

So, I did. I started reading even more and writing and then applying what I read. That is when our sales started to increase, our performance improved, and we started to really help the customer. I have sold my entire career. As I focused on doing the right things at the right time with the right people, my sales and career took off. So will yours. My success in sales is still ongoing and progressing. I have led and built sales teams, advised multinational companies on how to grow and train their sales teams, created new sales strategies for multiple clients and employers, and most important, coached sales champions. Once I began to care, everything changed.

So, while I have been there, it isn't the deciding factor in my life. Where I am going is much more important. It is the same for you as well.

Where are you going?
Your background is where you have been. The only thing that matters is where you are going. You can choose to be as successful as you desire.

The purpose of this book is to help you grow from where you are to where you want to be. It is about turning a dream into a desire, into a commitment, into reality. Knowing what you want is half the battle. Next, you need to know how to get there so you can grow.

If you sell anything ever, this is the book for you. If you care enough, you can sell.

"If you work hard enough, assert yourself, and **use your mind** and imagination, you can shape the world to your desires."

- MALCOLM GLADWELL

You are a reflection
of your choices.

Life always has been and always will be about choices.

The choice of the ideas we believe, the choice of the actions we take, the choice of the people we embrace, and the choice of the feelings we hold on to.

Our choices lead to actions and actions determine outcomes.

As a sales professional, the entire focus is to help people get what they actually need and want. You do that by helping others make better choices.

Those who care the most, show it through their actions.
Those who care the most, sell the most.

"To **be yourself** in a world
that is constantly trying
to make you something
else is the greatest
accomplishment."

—RALPH WALDO EMERSON

Your vision of **who you really are** is the only thing that **really matters**.

Without a destination, you will never get there. You are greater than you think you are. Your potential is unlimited.

Every salesperson with a pulse can make enough income to survive. But that is not why you are in sales. You are in sales to be the best, to give the best, to serve the best, and to create the best, and to change people's lives.

In the business world, most people don't want the best. They want to be protected. They want security. They want to keep their job, so they can pay their mortgage. They are not willing to take the risk to be great. Too many people accept mediocrity. That is why those who strive for greatness are so revered, so rewarded. A little excellence goes a long way.

"When you're committed to something, you will do what is required for the attainment of that thing. You'll stop wondering and start building. You'll stop being distracted and start learning. You'll start connecting. You'll start failing. You'll get what you want, rather than have a long list of 'ambitions.' You'll have actual accomplishments that reflect your inner goals and values. Your external environment will reflect your deepest internal views and aims."

—BENJAMIN HARDY

The path you create is your own.

Your life path is something unique that you create; it is organic – not linear.

There is a purpose and meaning for your life. Find it, embrace it, live it.

Thinking that "things" bring fulfillment is the reason the world is so full of quiet desperation.

Connect your "doings" to your purpose, and everything gets better. Alignment is key.

Believe in yourself first, act on your belief, and the results will come.

"Fear comes from a lack of knowledge. Accelerate your learning, **eliminate your fear**."

—JAY SHETTY

Fear is real. Deal with it.

When you have (feel) fear, try this 5-step plan:

1. *EMBRACE* the Fear – Think about every possibility. Write down the worst thing that can happen. This scenario should be the worst case possible. Accept this scenario as your starting point.

2. *DEFINE* the Fear – Be able to understand WHY you are afraid. Know thyself. Be true to yourself. Take the time to figure out your fear and motivations. Label and define them.

3. *QUESTION* the Fear – Ask yourself: Is this fear good, or is the fear bad? Does this fear motivate me, or does it paralyze me? Is this fear even real? What does it mean?

4. *CREATE* an ACTION PLAN – Create a step-by-step plan that will take you to your destination. Make sure to leave room for mistakes along the way. Each action you plan helps to lead you away from the worst-case scenario.

5. *TAKE ACTION* now – Nothing beats doing. Nothing. Action erases all fear. Follow your plan and adjust as you go.

As a bonus, action creates success, and success creates motivation. It is a cycle. Start pedaling.

"Strong-minded people **have**
a dedication that comes from
a **purpose in alignment** with
their deepest values."

—LARAE QUY

Quiet Down

Nobody likes to be told to be quiet, or to be calm, or to shut up.

It doesn't matter though: be quiet!

Meditation works. Pondering works. Prayer works.

When we are quiet and think, and when we express our feelings from inside and share them with our creator, with the higher power, we can connect with our purpose and potential.

Take time for prayer, pondering, or meditation every single day. When we do take time to gain understanding of our personal experiences, we learn about ourselves and our purpose. Tom English, a UK-based transformation mentor and leadership coach, exhorts us to learn that: *"The extent to which each person's program of learning in life is tailored to their needs and potential is quite incredible. Each individual is unique, and each has so much to offer."*

"We make a living by what
we get, but we **make a life** by
what we give."

—WINSTON CHURCHILL

Give, give again, then **give more**.

Karma is real.

The best-performing salespeople are those who are customer-centric, those who truly put their customers' interests first. That includes giving.

Be generous.
Share for sharing's sake.
Give your time, your ideas, your effort.

The funny thing about giving is that the more you give, the more you will have, and the happier you become.

Basic undeniable truth: The more you give, the more you will always have.

Also...

Giving helps you build trust.
Giving helps you build a reputation.

With a good reputation, anything is possible; you can sell on that.

"Shifting your focus from **getting** to **giving** is not only a nice way to live life and conduct business, but a very profitable way as well."

—JOHN DAVID MANN & BOB BURG

⑦
How to **Help Others**

There are two ways to help others.

1. Give them what they want and need.
2. Show kindness.

Showing kindness is the ultimate way to help others. It might be physical, it might be a smile, it might be an encouraging word, it might be providing protection, or it might be teaching. All service and help can be traced back to a foundation of kindness.

Dale G. Renlund teaches that: *"Not throwing stones is the first step in treating others with compassion. The second step is to try to catch stones thrown by others."*

And once we have decided to be kind, act with compassion, and to serve and help, we *NEED TO STOP*:

STOP letting the opinions of others determine how we feel.
STOP making excuses.
STOP waiting.
STOP listening to our fears.
STOP refusing help from others.

You have enough outside pressure, so take action without any inner inhibitions.

"You can't **take** care of anyone else unless you first take care of yourself. The good news is that we have more **control** than most **of** us realize. Each day is filled with thousands of **opportunities** to change the story of our lives."

—MICHAEL HYATT

Voluntary Enslavement?

If you don't own your time, you will always be a slave to the clock.

Planning works best. Always know what you should be doing at every moment.

Chunk your day. Create time periods (chunks) to accomplish specific tasks. Then do the tasks without allowing for distraction. That's right: You allow distractions. No one distracts you.

Follow a weekly plan, but create a new schedule every night for the next day. Always do the most important things first.

It may be exercise, it may be reading; it may be playing with your kids, it may be prayer, or it may be eating... Whatever it is, schedule it out, follow the schedule, and you will get so much more done.

"Now is the time to rescue lost dreams, rejuvenate our emotions, do the simple things that give us pleasure, and direct the scripts of our own stories. Now is the time to establish strategies to celebrate life."

—AUGUSTO CURY

9

Establish **Good Habits**

1. **Develop clarity** – In other words, know and decide what you want. Get clear on who you are and what you want to become by writing it down. When you have clear intentions and a focused purpose, your "why" becomes your main motivator. No action or sacrifice is too much for that goal. Review your purpose weekly. Review your actions daily.

2. **Start small** – Doing something over and over makes it easy. If you want to sell better, start by creating conversations. Don't focus on the sale itself – focus on the habit of picking up the phone and talking to people. Every big habit is supported by many smaller habits. Find the small habit and develop that first. It's easy to do many little things over and over again.

3. **Focus on routine** – Eventually, you'll be able to do those things on autopilot. Make your desired habit part of your daily routine. Write it down. Check it off your list. If you want better clients, find out what you need to do to get them, and then create habits that revolve around those specific actions. Calendar it into your daily schedule. Any goal is possible. Just commit to it (and write it down!).

4. **Reward desired behavior** – Bad habits get rewarded; if they didn't, you wouldn't have them. Don't change the reward – just change how it's applied. Find rewards that have meaning to you and use them to connect good behavior to desired outcomes.

5. **Journal your progress** – Celebrate wins. Contemplate mistakes. Create plans to magnify the win column and strategies to minimize the mistakes. Without proper reflection, the habits do not have any meaning. By applying your own personal meaning, you can accelerate your progress.

6. **Find your super supporter** – You need to spend time around the people who will help you keep your habits. Don't take it from me; take it from Oprah Winfrey, who once said, "Surround yourself with only people who are going to lift you higher." Find the most positive person you know and ask them to hold you accountable. They will make sure you are on track, and they will do it in a positive way. This type of supporter is needed to help you know that you are staying consistent with your values and that your actions align with your "why."

Habits help you do things consistently, without thinking about the entire process all the time. Habits can make or break you. The good thing is habits can be changed. The choices you make today form your habits of tomorrow. If you believe in your ability to adjust and change, you can develop habits that will enable you to maximize your potential.

"If you have trust with somebody, it can survive any downturn, any mistake, any problem. And if you don't have trust, it won't matter how good the business is. It will fall apart eventually."

—MARCUS LEMONIS

10

Develop an **Outward Mindset** (read the book too!)

Think about others more. Think about them as humans, not objects.

An inward mindset limits your possibilities and negatively affects your behavior. Your behavior is what determines all of your success, both professionally and personally.

An inward mindset is not introspection. We all need to be self-aware. An inward mindset is thinking about yourself and your needs rather than about the needs of others.

When you view and treat others as humans and not objects, every single relationship you have gets better. You will know how to treat them. You will know how to make them happy and how to help them accomplish their goals.

Anytime you're self-conscious or selfish, you are wrong. Whenever you are thinking about others, you will always be right.

Going from an inward mindset to an outward mindset is more than just making minor behavioral adjustments. It requires a shift in how we see and think about others. Our definition of reality determines how we respond to others. Therefore, how we treat others is not about them or their actions; it is 100% a reflection of what is happening deep inside of us.

Don't fixate on the shortcomings of your team, your clients, or your prospects. You have enough of your own.

As The Arbinger Institute teaches, the process of developing an outward mindset is simple:

1. **See:** See the needs of others.

2. **Adjust:** Adjust your actions to match those needs.

3. **Report:** Hold yourself accountable for your actions, your relationships, and especially for your thoughts and behavior.

Having an outward mindset allows you to truly see others for who they are. You can see their needs and fulfill them. Developing an outward mindset is the fastest way to develop trust.

"Success doesn't **measure** a **human** being, **effort** does."

—ADAM GRANT

Care + Effort =
Results

When you care enough and work hard enough, your results will be more than enough.

Caring is not empathy. Caring requires action. Caring requires you to check in. Caring is more than understanding and feeling; it is doing. The doing is what sets you apart. When someone feels cared for, they will trust you. When you care, you can sell.

"I put zero weight into
anyone's opinion about me,
because **I know** exactly
who I am."

—GARY VAYNERCHUK

Talk to yourself.

The key driver of self-image is what we tell ourselves about our past, present, and future.

Our self-talk becomes our personal stories. We believe what we tell ourselves.

Self-talk combined with matching action is the No. 1 way to change your life.

While I am no guru, I know that these are the stories you must tell yourself:

1. **"I treat others the way they want to be treated."**
   By treating others the way they want to be treated, my own personal fulfillment grows. I give respect and provide service. I show love, care, compassion, and consideration. I help others feel appreciated. I let others know they are important, that they matter, and that they are valuable. By valuing others, my confidence increases.

2. **"I am ever grateful."**
   Gratitude allows happiness to come into my life. I choose to show appreciation for what I have, whom I know, what I can learn, and whom I can help. I define and talk about the things I am grateful for on a daily basis. I know that the No. 1 way for me to be happy

is to choose to be grateful. The more thanks I show, the more my confidence increases.

3. **"I am accountable."**
I am reliable. I am responsible. I never blame others. I never make excuses. I take ownership of my successes as well as my mistakes. I know that my own performance is a direct result of what I think and the actions I take. By taking full responsibility daily, my confidence increases.

4. **"I believe in myself."**
When I fail, I learn. My failures are temporary because my perseverance is permanent. I push forward at all times because I know I can succeed. As I continually believe in myself, my confidence increases.

5. **"I have high standards."**
I do not let mediocrity enter my life. I am honest. I do not apologize for striving for excellence. My quality of life is a reflection of my high standards. I rise and lift others with me. By living up to my personal high standards, my confidence increases.

6. **"I follow my heart."**
Time is precious, and everyone has something that they are passionate about. I do what makes me and those around me happy. The cost of not following my heart is too great; I am going to live life with no regrets. As I follow my heart, my confidence increases.

7. **"I trust my gut."**
I value my intuition, since it is based on my subconscious mind and conscious mind working in harmony. I know what is true, and I know

what I want to be true. I trust my gut feelings, my inner voice. As I trust myself, my confidence increases.

8. **"I am resilient."**
   I have overcome many challenges and will overcome many more. The times that are the toughest are the times I learn the most. I never back down. I work hard and I push through. As I act in a resilient manner, my confidence increases.

9. **"I help people."**
   I matter because I make a difference. While I may get tired, I am not weary. I share myself and love to serve. By making a difference, my confidence increases.

If we tell ourselves our personal truth enough, it manifests into reality. Our reality and our actions will always match the story we believe.

"Marketing and sales isn't about trying to persuade, coerce, or manipulate people into buying your services. It's about putting yourself out in front of, and offering your services to, those whom you are meant to serve – **people** who already **need** and are looking for **your services**."

—MICHAEL PORT

Win Today

To win in sales and in life all you need to do is win the day.

If you win the day, you are a success. Win a few days in a row and you are a true winner.

Win more days than you lose and you will be unstoppable.

Here is how to win the day, every day:

1.   Write down what you want (goals).
2.   Write down who you are (values, principles).
3.   Take one step, one massive action toward your goals as aligned with your principles.
4.   Learn something new (listen, read, study).
5.   Help someone.
6.   Thank someone.
7.   Exercise.
8.   Erase excuses (no blaming, full accountability).
9.   Reflect on your day and create an action plan for tomorrow.

Every day that you do these nine things, you will win. So, go win today. And go win tomorrow, too. And as you win, you learn that you can keep winning.

If you care enough to win, others will care enough to help you on your journey.

"Amateurs sit and wait for inspiration, the rest of us just get up and go to work."

—STEPHEN KING

Excuses are painful.

**Failure hurts. Excuses cause lasting failure.
Excuses are just bad stories.**

We believe the stories we tell ourselves. Excuses create the hardship.
Excuses create the pain. If you let go of excuses, you will find tremendous
joy and strength. The more excuses you have, the more problems you
seem to have. The more excuses you find, the less in control you feel. Your
excuses are ruining you. Your excuses are hurting you. The only thing you
need to do is stop creating them.

If the excuses do not exist, then you don't have to worry about believing
them. Ownership erases excuses. Own your beliefs, values, and actions.
Once you own yourself, there are no more excuses. No excuses = no
more false stories. Now you can live up to your true potential.

"The harsh truth is that those in sales and sales leadership who understand and **master the basics** thrive, and those who ignore them perpetually struggle."

—MIKE WEINBERG

Everybody Sells

Some people just don't admit it.

If you have to share an idea, persuade, inspire, motivate, or lead (which is everybody), you are in sales.

The question is, do you accept that you are in sales?

"A person's **success** in life **can** usually **be measured** by the number of uncomfortable conversations he or she is willing to have."

—TIM FERRIS

(16)

In **sales**, you **make** as much **money** as you want.

Professional sales is the only "job" where (if you are with the right company or working for yourself) your pay is an accurate reflection of your performance. Embrace sales and your life will get better.

"To sell well is to convince someone else to part with resources – not to deprive that person, but to leave him better off in the end. This is what it means to **serve**: improving another's life and, in turn, improving **the world**."

—DAN PINK

'Tis Nothin' Nobler

It doesn't matter how you look, or where you come from – the profession of sales is the great equalizer.

Trust me, I would know.

Sales isn't sleazy. Some salespeople are, though.

Sales is a job where you have to prove your worth every day. Sales is painful, sales is hard, sales is rewarding, sales is gratifying, and sales is not about you. It is about what you do for and with others.

Sales is the ability to help people. Sales is taking destiny into your own hands.

Sales is the ability to influence and impact.

To be great in sales, you need to be smart, hardworking, caring, curious, and creative.

Be proud of what you do. Be proud of the skills you have and will develop.

As you honor your craft, respect the role as a professional helper, and your confidence and sales will grow.

"The only way you can
uncover and drive real
urgency is to truly
understand what the
priorities of the people you
are selling to are and what
they're trying to accomplish.
Once you uncover them,
you need to show them how
your solution can help them
get there faster than their
existing plans will or more
effectively."

—JOHN BARROWS

(18)

To **be great** in sales... don't be salesy.

You don't need to be an extrovert.

You don't need to be a smooth talker.
You don't have to be good at selling to sell well.
You don't have to be a sales person to be great at sales.

You just have to choose to help people.

Just like Jeffrey Gitomer says: *"Great salespeople are relationship builders who provide value and help their customers win."*

Just care.

"I'm intrigued that the same letters from the alphabet are used in the word **silent** and in the word **listen**. Perhaps it's evidence that the most important part of listening involves remaining silent."

—ROBERT HERJAVEC

3 Traits **All** Top Performers Share

Top performers are curious. No exceptions.

Curiosity is driven by care and concern.

If you don't possess these three traits, stop selling now (or develop them):

1. Desire to understand. (humility)
2. Listening skills with intent to understand.
3. Ability to connect understanding with relevant opportunities, solutions, and insights.

"If you can't **explain it simply**, you don't **understand it well** enough."

—ALBERT EINSTEIN

20

Speak Easy

Speak words in a way that makes sense to you and to your clients.

It is always better to speak simply than to try to sound smart.

It is always better to say, "You won't ever need to worry again," rather than, "We reduce risk."

It is always better to say, "Your kids are going to love it here!" rather than, "Families enjoy this resort."

It is always better to say, "You will know where everything is, in real-time," rather than, "You will have increased product visibility."

Say it in a way that is natural for you, and most important, makes an emotional connection with them.

"Customers don't want to be coerced, controlled, or otherwise pushed around. They **value authentic relationships** based on transparency, competence, credibility, and trust, and they'll pay more for those qualities, even in today's difficult selling environment."

—STEVE ANDERSEN

21

The ONLY 6 Things Your
Clients NEED to Believe

The simplest and most impactful true piece of sales strategy and training I have ever received comes from one of my mentors, Steve Andersen, Founder of Performance Methods, Inc. and author of *Beyond The Sales Process.*

Steve Andersen expertly teaches that your partners and prospects need to believe you have the BEST:

1. **Product** – The customer believes your products are superior to your competitors' products.
2. **Resources** – The customer believes your resources will enable their success.
3. **Expertise** – The customer believes your people will provide expertise/best practices.
4. **Services** – The customer believes your service levels are higher and more proactive.
5. **Industry Experience** – The customer believes your experience with similar customers reduces risk.
6. **Brand/Reputation** – The customer believes in your reputation for quality, service and excellence, and your organization derives competitive advantage as a result.

So, in summary, your clients and prospects need to believe that your product:

- Is superior (technology, quality, functionality).
- Will reduce risk (previous success).
- Will enable success (solution, new insights, growth) and that you and your company provide the best and easiest experience.

That is all. Show this, prove this, and live this, and you will create unlimited business for life.

"Sellers have lost their way because they've forgotten that **it's really all about the customer**—their needs, their agenda, their business case, their preferred channels of communication. Timeless value must be combined with modern techniques to break through and succeed in helping customers; saving them from their apathy."

—TONY J. HUGHES

22

To **really help**, the prospect must be encouraged to grow, challenged to change, and shown the way.

To do this, the sales professional (you) must actively teach and share commercial insights with all prospects and customize the sales process (be flexible).

- **Teach** – This is where you teach about the industry, about your solution, and about possible options that are derived from insights that show potential for previously unknown opportunities to have the biggest impact.

- **Adapt** – Find out how they buy and structure your process to help them buy better and more easily.

If you can do these two things properly, you will be able to help create true value and will never be seen as a commodity or worse, a "vendor."

"Respect what's valuable for
your customers and focus
on their preferences first.
When it comes to value, the
customers' perspectives
matter."

—TAMARA SCHENK

23

Labels

Just like your customers and partners need to believe a few things about you, your product, and your company, you also need to believe a few things.

You need to believe that:

1. You deserve success.
2. You will create your own success.
3. You are persistent, patient, and helpful.

Those are the labels you must own.

Why? Because they are true.
We always believe the labels we allow to be placed upon us.

"No misfortune is so bad that whining about it won't make it worse."

—JEFFREY R. HOLLAND

24

More labeling

How you label others is exactly how you will treat them.

How you feel about your clients is your label of them.

How you label every situation is what the situation becomes.

Perception turns into reality based on your own definitions and labels.

Be careful with your labels; they usually come true.

"Law of the Universe:
Nothing happens until
something moves.

Law of Business: Nothing
happens until someone sells
something."

—JEB BLOUNT

25

The **foundational** **basics** of all sales (and marketing) ...

A	*Attention*
I	*Interest*
D	*Desire*
A	*Action*

When you get their attention, spark interest (value), instill desire (benefits, future state, outcomes), and motivate them to take action (trust, pain, results), then you can help others make better decisions.

Marketing and sales must be unified. They must be united for the same common purpose of growing revenue by helping buyers make better decisions. As marketing guru, SaaS founder, and best-selling author Sangram Vajre evangelizes: *"The Value of Marketing is Defined by Sales."*

Sales is simple. Sales is the willingness and ability to help others get what they want by making good buying decisions.

"A trusted referral and a personal connection seal the deal...**every single day**."

—JOANNE BLACK

26

People buy from those they **like** and **trust**. (...if they provide true value first.)

The barrier to "like" is super low. Really, it means they just can't hate you or find you off-putting.

First steps: Listen more than you talk (60/40 is a good number), have good hygiene, and think about others.

The fastest way to earn trust is having someone vouch for you. That is a referral. If you can get someone to refer you to someone else, the trust is now in place.

Referrals are the fastest way to sales growth.

There are a lot of other ways to earn trust as well; none as easy as a referral, though.

You need to be trusted both for your integrity (morality, honesty) and your competence (skills, abilities, knowledge). What you say, how you talk, the questions you ask, and how you act all start the process of building trust.

People buy from those they like and trust, with trust being far more important.

When you make it about them, when you care and are curious, building trust becomes easier.

"**1)** Focus on what customers need, not what you want to sell (there is a difference),

2) Try to establish some sort of relationship first (it's just like networking; give long before you hope to receive), and

3) Learn to connect people and in turn they will connect you."

—JEFF HADEN

(27)

Always Be Helping. If you aren't helping, you shouldn't be selling.

Be helpful. Expect nothing. Work for everything.

In order to help better, just care more.

Always be helping could also just be: *Always Be Caring*

"**Questions** create conversations,

Conversations build relationships,

Relationships develop opportunities and

Opportunities lead to sales."

—PHIL M. JONES

28

All of the new psychology, research, and techniques in the world won't help you if you can't **apply them in real life**.

Great salespeople are client-focused. They need to know how to have great conversations.

They know how to listen. You need to be able to understand your client. Great salespeople know what questions to ask, when to ask them, and what the answers mean. They can apply those answers to a client's needs and wants and craft meaningful solutions.

If you only learn one skill, learn how to ask the right questions the right way. And SHUT UP!

Yes, learn to shut up and listen, too.

"**We need each other more than we know**. Build authentic relationships and it can change your life (it has mine). We don't do anything great in this world alone."

—KIMBERLY DAVIS

(29)

Human (Emotional) Needs

Tony Robbins teaches that these are the 6 Emotional Human Needs we all have:

1. **Certainty** – The need for security, stability, and reliability.

2. **Variety/Uncertainty** – The need for change, stimulation, and challenge.

3. **Significance** – The need to feel acknowledged, recognized, and valued.

4. **Love/Connection** – The need to love and to feel loved, to feel a connection with others.

5. **Growth** – The need to grow, improve, and develop, both in character and in spirit.

6. **Contribution** – The need to give, to help others, and to make a difference.

Each one of us has all six needs.

Yet, each person has a dominant need or two.

"Being affirmed by someone
is a great feeling. We never
know our **impact** on another,
especially **the ones who need
it the most**."

—MICHAEL DAVID CHAPMAN

(30)

Influencing Others

Robert Cialdini's book, *Influence*, is the greatest resource produced so far on learning the various methods for how people can be influenced.

These are Cialdini's "6 Principles of Influence":

1. **Reciprocity** – People tend to return a favor, thus the large amounts of free samples in marketing. Do something for someone, and they will often do something for you.

2. **Commitment and Consistency** – If something is consistently heard or seen, it is more likely to be believed and acted upon. Also, if people commit to a goal, they are more likely to honor that commitment even if the original reward or incentive is taken away after they have already agreed.

3. **Social Proof** – People will do things that they see other people do or approve of.

4. **Authority** – People generally obey authority figures if they deem that authority legitimate.

5. **Liking** – People are persuaded by other people that they like. If Peyton Manning or Beyoncé likes something, we tend like it is as well.

6. **Scarcity** – Scarcity will generate demand since we think it must be valuable if it is running out.

These are valid and scientifically-backed principles. To learn how to influence, study those six methods.

"**Success is** not about what you do; it is about how you do it. Meaning that success is **a choice**, the strategies, and techniques that successful professionals use to get ahead are available to all of us."

—MERIDITH ELLIOT POWELL

31

The Complete Impact Model

To truly create an impact on someone, you must be able to persuade them to get more of what they want and need in life.

That is sales. That is why we sell: to help others.

The complete impact model is very simple to explain, but it takes serious dedication and skill to apply.

The first step is to discover what their main human need is. You need to truly care enough about them to get to know them. Find out what drives them. Learn which of Tony Robbins' 6 Human Needs they are most connected to.

The second step is once you know what they are motivated by, you can then determine what principle of influence you are going to use to help them make a positive decision. You choose a Cialdini influence method and then combine with their main human need and do it in an ethical fashion.

**Basic Human Need + Influence Principle
= Complete Impact**

"Life is not fair; it never was,
and it isn't now. Do not fall
into the trap...The entitlement
trap, of feeling like you're
a victim. You are not. Give
thanks. Appreciate what you
do have...the more we give
thanks, the more we receive
to be thankful for. Gratitude
is the gift that always gives
back. It's a scientific fact that
gratitude reciprocates."

—MATTHEW MCCONAUGHEY

32

The **10 Rules** For Better Sales Experiences

1. Always own your results. Today's. Not yesterday's.
2. Listen more than you talk.
3. Follow up, more than you think is needed, and faster, too.
4. Get your partners (clients) to keep commitments; the better the commitment, the better the partnership.
5. Do not talk badly about others.
6. Build trust through action.
7. The best questions always win.
8. Do not fake anything.
9. Show gratitude and appreciate the good in others.
10. Bring extreme positive energy to everything you do and everyone you meet.

"**People are interested in** outcomes; **your product** is just the way of obtaining it."

—ANTHONY IANNARINO

33

Systems are better than processes.

Some salespeople sell better than others. Yet, it is not the process they use. It is the system.

Yes, the best ones follow a system. Systems are flexible while processes aren't. Not always in the same order, the system they follow is pretty clear across any industry.

The sales professional must be able to:
1. Talk to the right people.
2. Understand and emphasize the pain and goals.
3. Explain, show, and differentiate value (insights and solutions).
4. Provide a map of/to the future.
5. Get buy-in (consensus, commitments, approval).

Most salespeople can do a few of these things. Care more by mastering all five.

If you can do all five of these things well, you can create new business forever.

"The process of becoming
a top performer requires
constant learning and
personal reflection."

—LEE BARTLETT

34

Characteristics of **the** **Best** Sales Professionals

If you have them, focus on developing them more fully.

If you don't have them, develop them, and then focus on developing them more fully.

1. **Achievement-oriented**
2. **Deep curiosity**
3. **Humble** – The best are confident. You need to be confident. Confidence is not arrogance. Humility allows you to learn and grow. The more humble you are as a sales professional, the more you will learn and the more people will like you.
4. **Resilience** – NO cannot faze you. NO cannot hurt you. NO is not you.
5. **Never be embarrassed** – (lack of self-conscious). If you are humble and curious and care about others, your own embarrassment will not be a factor. You are always trying to get better no matter how it looks or how you are perceived.
6. **Duty** – You are reliable. You are accountable. You get the job done and people trust you.

You determine your success. Not only who you are, but what you do.

"Never **make a** permanent **decision** based on a temporary emotion."

—JUSTIN BARISO

35

When navigating the stormy seas of sales, you need extreme composure.

Use the 7 Cs of Sales to develop and maintain your professional composure.

The 7 Cs of Sales:

1. **Communication** – No matter what else is in place, if the message is not understood, nothing ever happens. Clarity and simplicity must be the root of your communication. No relationships are formed, and no value is ever shared without solid communication. This is the foundation of all sales.

2. **Care** (includes curiosity, compassion, and craftsmanship) – While not the foundation, this is the #1 most important characteristic of great sales professionals. No one cares about you until they know how much you care about them. When you care, you will do anything and everything to become better and to help others. Your care for the problem and for the customer is driven by humility.

   - *Curiosity:* The desire to understand and learn erases most skill-gaps. Curiosity is what allows you to understand others and the situation and see the big picture. Curiosity means you are humble enough to learn, which means you are humble enough to help.

- *Compassion:* This is what drives you to help others.

- *Craftsmanship:* When you care, you will do whatever it takes to become the best in your field; you will develop the skills, abilities, and knowledge you need. When you are a master of your craft, your message will be clear, and your results and effort will be trusted.

3. **Character** – True character is about being honest, keeping your word, sharing truth, being transparent, aligning your goals, and not having to remember what you said. Winning relationships are fortified by strong character.

4. **Confidence** – You need to instill confidence in others. They need to believe that you and your product (service) will help them gain value, reduce risk, and reduce costs. This is about taking action and showing enthusiasm. No amount of skill can make up for lack of action. Passion incites confidence. Confidence is an emotion as well as an action.

5. **Courage** – Your ability to say what needs to be said and to do what needs to be done at the right time is how you display courage. It won't be easy to tell someone they are wrong, or their idea won't work, but being courageous is what allows space for growth. You know what must be done. You know the right way to do things, and taking the right action is the only way to show courage.

6. **Creativity** – Boring doesn't get remembered. Be creative to create an impression. Boring is hard work. Engage your team, your client, and your prospects by doing things differently. When mundane activities become new and fresh, they are much easier to embrace. Creativity creates excitement and buy-in.

7. **Commitment** – When you get others to keep commitments, everyone improves. Keeping commitments is the only way relationships progress. Actions need to happen for change to take place. Keep your commitments and help others keep theirs.

When I learned these, my life changed. So did my career. So will yours.

Everything you do needs to be wrapped in value.

Everything you say must be pointed in one direction, and that is giving other people what they want, need, and aspire to be.

If you can remember to master the 7 Cs of Sales, you will change your life and the life of so many others.

"The way customers research and buy today demands changes in how you sell. **No longer can you focus on just your actions**. Today, the sales process has to be collaborative. It's about finding the FIT early in the process, and then helping your prospect gain comfort with your ability to help them achieve results."

—IAN ALTMAN

You are in sales for one main purpose: to **help others** get what they want.

The best way to do that is through partnerships, trusted partnerships. The strongest relationship is one where all sides are committed to the same objective, where everyone is aligned to the same goals.

You need to move on from vendor – supplier relationships where you are reactive and only servicing a need, to one of true partnership. This type of relationship is where you are more than valued, but you are trusted as well.

The legendary EVP from SalesForce – Warren Wick – teaches that: *"Your customer needs a deep relationship with you. Your time and investment in building trust will pay dividends as you weather the storms of a long sales cycle. When you put their challenges at the center of your focus and provide real solutions, you'll start to develop aligning interests. You have to take not only an interest in their business and problems, but also in the people. As you truly look out for your clients' best interests – like you would for friends or family – you'll eventually end up solving your own challenge as well: achieving your sales goals."*

Build a partnership. Partnership is when you search and create new opportunities together. That is exciting. That is when selling becomes incredible, inspiring, and fun.

In order to do that, you must first give them what they need so you can give them what they want. Do it over and over again. Be consistent with your execution and helpful with your insights. The last step is also the first step: Always be transparent and vulnerable with your goals, purpose, strengths, and weaknesses. Trust is built in the aftermath of vulnerability.

"**Art** can't be hurried. It **must be allowed** to take its course. It must be given its **space** – and can't be rushed or checked off a to-do list on the way to something else."

—RYAN HOLIDAY

(37)

Do you like crafting?

If you don't have a craft, don't worry; it's never too late.

If you truly want to be a better salesperson, a better speaker, a better leader, a better writer, a better professional, a better anything, or even just a better person, you need to study YOUR craft.

Take pride in your work. Be the best you can be. Develop all of your talents.

This takes effort. This takes time. Study books. Read, read more, then read even more. Ask questions. Find a mentor. Become an expert in what you do.

Jon Gordon says: *"Be so invested in your craft that you don't have time to listen to the critics and naysayers. No time for negativity. You're too busy creating your future."*

Honor your craft and it will always serve you.

If you want to become a professional, to actually live the life you were meant to: take action, do more. Always be doing. And while you are "doing" also read *Turning Pro* and *The War of Art* by Steven Pressfield. (These two books will inspire and empower you.)

"Humility is the awareness that there's a lot you don't know and that a lot of what you think you know is distorted or wrong."

—DAVID BROOKS

38

Your **craft** is your **art**.

Your profession is sales. Your craft is service. Master the art of helping.

Your work is to create masterpieces of trust and value. Don't rush it. Pay attention to the details. Do your best and practice often. When you think about others and stay humble, your experience will turn into art.

As you work hard and focus on others your craft becomes your calling. Whenever you ponder if pursuing your calling is worth it, remember what Jeff Goins teaches:

"I used to think that your calling was about doing something good in this world. Now I understand it's about becoming someone good—and letting that goodness impact the world around you."

When you become someone good, your craft enables you to lift those around you. That is when you craft turns into your art and you live your calling.

"**Pride** is concerned with who is right.

Humility is concerned with what is right."

—EZRA TAFT BENSON

39

Pride Kills Sales.

There are two types of pride.

1. **Pride for/in others: good.**
2. **Pride for yourself: bad.**

When you have pride, you think you are better than others. You won't change, because your way works or has worked in the past. You are unteachable. You are right, and everyone else is wrong.

Pride also kills relationships.

We all know that the enemy of greatness is ego. Drop the ego by reminding yourself daily to look at things from new angles and from new perspectives.

Think about others and their experiences, and your experience becomes so much more valuable.

"You, the salesperson, have the ability to **have better conversations with the customer**.

The question is, are you willing to do it?

Are you willing to spend more time with your customer? Are you willing to slow down in order to speed up?"

—VICTOR ANTONIO

Throw away your presentation.

Have a conversation first. Never present until you know enough to create a personalized experience.

As Leslie Venetz teaches: *"Address the unique needs of your prospect and explain how your product can solve those specific challenges. Frankly, few prospects care about the parts of your presentations that don't speak directly to them."*

Be unique. Don't be boring. In order to get noticed, you need to BE WORTH NOTICING. Do something different. If you have to be told how to do it, you are boring. Figure it out. Try something. Try anything. Everyone values real conversation. No one likes being sold to or talked at. We all crave connection. Connect more. Show you care by connecting your solution to their desired outcomes.

"Know the other person's agenda and help them accomplish it."

—ANDREW SOBEL

We all have some desires.

We all have some of the same desires.

While they might be expressed in different ways, when you understand what drives people to do what they do, you can help them get what they want.

We all have the desire to be creative and in control.
We all should have the desire to improve ourselves and those around us.

Use those desires to help others make better buying decisions.

"The fastest way to develop yourself is to find a mentor or hire a coach who has the experience and expertise to accelerate your learning process. Behavior change is hard, but you can do it."

—ALICE HEIMAN

Seriously, you need more skills!

These are some important skills to learn:

- *Learn* to hold/conduct a meeting. (State objective, let others speak, drive to decision, delegate assignments, and restate next steps.)

- *Learn* to tell a story.

- *Learn* to listen. (Truly listen, feed back the content and feeling of the other's words, confirm you heard correctly, ask a relevant follow-up question to further clarify your understanding of their situation, eventually tell a story and/or give examples of similar situations.)

- *Learn* to ask questions.

- *Learn* to help others make and keep commitments.

- *Learn* to follow up with encouragement.

"People don't believe what you tell them. They rarely believe what you show them. They often believe what their friends tell them.

They always believe what they tell themselves.

What leaders do:
They give people stories they can tell themselves. Stories about the future and about change."

—SETH GODIN

How To Tell A Story

When we tell each other a story, we connect, we feel, and we develop trust.

Humans were built to connect with stories. Stories are the way humans have learned and shared knowledge for thousands of years. Those who tell the best stories are seen as experts, in every situation.

In sales, the best stories always win.

While there are lots of keys and strategies to telling great stories, here are the main steps to a great story.

If you always follow these five main ideas, you will never tell a bad story again.

1. The story must be relevant to the audience.

2. You must be super passionate.

3. Always have a character who has a problem, who finds a guide, and who takes a journey that gets them to some type of resolution.

    a. The customer is the hero and the main character, always.

b. Never make yourself the hero. You can/should be the guide, however.

4. Start in the middle or at the climax and then work around it, never at the very beginning, and especially don't start with the end (then there would be no reason to listen to the story).

5. Finish by applying the message to their current situation.

This is for every type of story you tell, not just sales stories.

"Selling is all about serving others – and that includes your team members, managers and yourself as well as your customers.

It's about intention and contribution. It's about giving that which you want. You owe people that."

—BERNADETTE MCCLELLAND

When you are selling, everything you say should **have a purpose** and be valuable to the customer.

- Make the complex simple. Reduce the complexity and you will always be welcome.
- Share insights and opportunities. Be more valuable than Google.
- Teach them what is most important for success in their specific situation.
- Make sure what you say aligns with what they need and want first, and then goes beyond that to create new value that was previously never imagined.

To speak this way and to sell this way takes preparation. It takes focus. It takes thinking more about the customer than yourself.

Take the time to prepare and speak the right words with the right message at the right time.

"Enchantment is the purest form of sales. Enchantment is all about changing people's hearts, minds and actions because you **provide them a vision** or a way to do things better. The difference between enchantment and simple sales is that with enchantment you have the other person's best interests at heart, too."

—GUY KAWASAKI

This is the only thing you need to **memorize**...

Memorize your value statement. Don't worry about memorizing anything else.

The rest is conversation. Make this conversational because you know it so well that you can adapt it to any situation.

This is the structure: Character. Problem. Solution. Plan. Results.

Let's say you sell RFID equipment to manufacturing companies. You have tons of product lines and thousands of different solutions. So, you boil it down into one sentence.

Character: Manufacturing companies
Problem: Missing inventory
Solution: RFID
Plan: System to increase accountability
Results: True visibility, eliminate write-offs

Example:

"Manufacturing companies that are tired of expensive missing inventory use our patented RFID technology to build systems that increase accountability while providing true visibility that eliminates write-offs. They now know where the stuff actually is."

Your turn:

Create your VALUE STATEMENT.
(Character. Problem. Solution. Plan. Results.)

"Stay consistent and patient
in your prospecting, build
strong relationships, follow
up – trust me, you will reap
the rewards."

—RANA KORDAHI

Prospect: Your Life Depends On It

You cannot sell to people, clients, or customers who do not exist.

If you are not speaking with them, they do not exist. The only way to sell well and sell consistently is to prospect. Prospecting means calling people. It means asking for referrals. It means knocking on doors. Prospecting is the single task that creates the most success for any person in sales.

Those who don't prospect, fail. Once they begin to prospect, they succeed. It is a choice.

"What is a cynic?
A man who knows the price
of everything and the value of
nothing."

—OSCAR WILDE

In order to sell value, you need to **show value** first.

Consultative selling (asking questions and prescribing appropriate action) and insight selling (sharing new knowledge) work with an engaged buyer.

In order to get to that point, though, you must show value as soon as possible, as in from the very first 2-3 minutes of the first conversation. Don't waste their time by asking too many questions too early. Show them what the value is and then go back and learn how to tailor that value to their current situation, needs, and problems.

In the end, value-selling (showing and proving client-specific value, not just a generic solution) built on trusted relationships is the only method that always works and creates repeat business. And often, the most value is not found in solving current problems but in helping them to maximize new opportunities.

"Your success depends on how you **align your** personal **values** with the actions you take."

—SHAWN KAROL SANDY

People will hate you.

If you try to trick and negatively manipulate someone, they will hate you.

Never selfishly manipulate. You can influence and persuade. You can make it easier to buy from you by limiting options. You can support and encourage, but never trick or lie or bend the truth.

It is not worth it. When people hate you, they stop buying.

Plus, great salespeople don't lie. They don't need to, and they wouldn't do it anyway.

"In today's business world
– with the emphasis on
building lasting customer
relationships – it is
important to **help the
prospect determine if they
should buy**. To do this, the
salesperson needs to enable
the prospect to visualize how
their world would improve if
they acquired your product
or service capabilities."

—JULIE THOMAS

How To Introduce Yourself

You never get a second chance to make a great first impression. So keep the amount of talk about yourself to a minimum. Talk about them, and they will remember you.

Mike Weinberg, the author of *New Sales. Simplified.* teaches that these are the things you must say, usually in this order:

I head up / I run the... (sales, business development, the south region, etc.)

We help... (attorneys, medical device companies, CEOs, etc.)

Who are seeking a solution to solve... (late payments, missing inventory, increase brand awareness, etc.)

While looking to achieve... (increase cash on hand, true asset utilization, market leadership, etc.)

And tired of fighting... (with their clients, outdated systems, overpaid SEO consultants, etc.)

So they can...(grow more sales, get new clients, reduce costs, etc.)

Fill in the blanks with your specifics and your ability to open doors will increase.

"Your first objective in a sales
call should be to get the buyer
to tell you their stories, not
the other way around. If you
don't hear their stories first,
how will you know
which of your stories to tell?"

—PAUL SMITH

(50)

Your Customer's (Partner's) Value Story

If you can only tell one story, this is the one to tell.

Learn how to paint a picture of the client's current problems and goals. Inside that picture, show them the mistakes they need to avoid. Provide them with data and insights into what a better future would look like if they were able to become the hero in their own story. Then show them the way to get there. That is value; that is the story you must tell over and over.

Replace with your own custom phrases: When customers have *"this"* issue that creates *"this"* problem, they use our product to gain *"the desired result"* every day.

Example: When purchasing managers are tired of out-of-contract purchases that cause them to overpay for required services, they use Acme Contract Management Suite to reduce costs by maintaining 100% visibility to contract compliance.

"No longer do we have to be gregarious, objection-fighting machines **to be good at sales**. We can just tell stories about our experiences with the products or services. We can be there to answer questions from people who want to know more. This is what selling looks like today."

—CHRIS SPURVEY

(51)

Your product doesn't **matter**.

Well, it does, eventually.

But not in the beginning. Don't lead with your product. Lead with your customer's value story.

Product led growth is important. Your client's journey is more important.

"It's always critical to **engage** our **customers** in helping them understand the variety of issues that should be important to their decision."

—DAVID BROCK

Every conversation must be valuable.

It is not about you. It never was.

Every conversation must be earned. That is earned by presenting and sharing something of value to your client. It might be a new idea, or a different way of doing something, or exclusive industry information.

You could be diving into their processes to help them uncover missed opportunities, but no matter how you help, just make sure every conversation is something the customer perceives as valuable.

Humans connect with stories. We connect our past to our future with the stories we tell ourselves. We connect to others with the stories we listen to. Stories help us feel emotions and have the power to transform. The world's greatest teachers all teach/taught with stories.

"The best salespeople today
are not only skillful at
establishing trust
but are respectfully
assertive."

—SHARI LEVITIN

Push on the pain. It is the only way **to help**.

Everyone avoids pain.

We all run from pain faster than we run toward pleasure. In order to truly help, real sales professionals understand the power of pain and make sure the future partner also understands the pain they are dealing with.

Since pain is so hard to deal with, most people try to hide it and pretend it doesn't exist. Sales is about helping, and you can't hide pain; it needs to be exposed; it needs to be remedied. Until the pain is felt, no action will happen.

"Value is in the eyes of the customer. The customer doesn't always readily look in the right direction, so it's our job to **help them see** the entire picture."

—MARK HUNTER

Value always finds its way back to the wallet.

Professionals know how to show and explain value. They are not afraid to be authentic. When you share true value, you need to monetize it, quantify it, and put a dollar amount on it.

If someone saves time, how much? What is that time worth each day, week, month, or year to the entire company?

Whenever you share value, monetize it. Don't expect them to do it themselves; teachers need to show. The greatest sales professionals are also the greatest teachers.

If you want to become a professional, you need to first stop being an amateur. Steve Pressfield in *Turning Pro* writes that: *"The amateur allows his worth and identity to be defined by others. The amateur craves third-party validation. The amateur is tyrannized by his imagined conception of what is expected of him. He is imprisoned by what he believes he ought to think, how he ought to look, what he ought to do, and who he ought to be."*

Yet, we all have the power to change, we can overcome amateurism and "Turn Pro" by becoming committed to our work and purpose.

Mr. Pressfield goes on to say: *"What we get when we turn pro is, we find our power. We find our will and our voice and we find our self-respect. We become who we always were but had, until then, been afraid to embrace and to live out."*

The more you find your voice and power, the more you can help others. The more you can help others, the more you can show you care. The more you show you care, the more you sell.

"**Trust** is equal parts
character and competence.
You can look at any
leadership failure, and it's
always a failure of one or the
other."

—STEPHEN M.R. COVEY

Insights Drive Partnerships.

Insights show competence and help build trust.

Insights are not just thought leadership; they are the application of the ideas.

Insights are not data and not facts; they are the meaning of the data, and what they can do with those facts that create insights. Insight is not visibility; it is showing them how to use the visibility to create new opportunities. An insight acknowledges what is true, changes the way someone thinks, and shows new, not-thought-of possibilities. If the insights you share help your clients accomplish their goals, you will create everlasting trust.

Trusted partnerships are the foundation for successful sales growth. Real growth that is based on trust comes when you take pain (challenges, learnings, mistakes) and mix in some reflection. Think about what happened and take action to fix those mistakes. Insights come from action and experience.

"People who add value to others do so intentionally. To add value, leaders must give of themselves, and that rarely occurs by accident. If you want to be the best leader you can possibly be, no matter how much or how little natural leadership talent you possess, you need to become a serving leader."

—JOHN C. MAXWELL

Give them what they want so you can give them what they need.

The great podcaster and sales thought leader Brian G. Burns teaches: *"Instead of doing more dumb things faster we need to learn to start conversations with strangers."*

If we care enough, we will start the right type of conversations. Conversations build trust. Once the conversation is started, then we can begin to help.

Trust can help overcome any setback. Trust is earned. Sometimes deals do not close. Sometimes sales do not happen. Often it is because of misalignment. You are not aligned with what they want. It doesn't matter what they need until they have what they want. So when a deal is stalled, when you have lost momentum, go back and have better conversations. Make sure you know what they want. Once you know, give it to them.

Give them what they want. Then they will not resent you for forcing something on them. They will trust you, and they will like you. Once they have what they want, give them what they need. That is when you begin to really sell.

"What if you let your
customers do the talking?"

—TRISH BERTUZZI

Treat them like family, but **better**.

We would do anything for our family. That is good.

We sometimes hurt the ones we love because we are careless. That is bad.

Be careful. Listen first.

Do anything for your clients, and always give them the respect and care they deserve and need.

Dr. Moshe Engelberg, the author of the transformative book *The Amare Wave,* teaches that with love we can transform business and relationships. First, we must accept the humanity of everyone we come in contact with and then act accordingly.

Moshe says that: *"In business, moral disengagement through dehumanization occurs when we reduce customers to market share to be captured, employees to assets to be deployed, and competitors to faceless enemies to be destroyed. We've been taught this is necessary in business. That is a lie. It is not. Really, it is simply fear taking form."*

If we let go of fear, we can learn to love. Care is love in action. Caring for others is how we bring love to our relationships and business to grow everyone's revenue.

"People who choose to unify
in an organization do not
obliterate their separateness.
Rather, joining together
into something beyond
their individual reach gives
their separateness new
purpose and meaning. Their
membership in something
larger pulls more energy from
them, causing an increase in
their functional capacities.
It's not just that they act
differently; their interior
purpose and experience is
transformed as well. They
take others into themselves
rather than keeping them out.
They expand."

—JIM FERRELL

Secret Sauce

You are the secret sauce.

Join with others and contribute. As you combine your skills and experience, everyone improves. No matter who you hire or outsource your work to, unless you are involved, it will not work as well as it could. Delegate but still supervise. In the end, all success and failure is your fault. Don't be absent. Know your worth and act accordingly. It is a journey and you are in control until you give it up.

Pay attention to the big picture and overall outcome as well as the details, and do it for as long as it takes to get there. You are the magic ingredient, so don't waste all your work by not being present when you are needed most. Sales, just like any relationship, cannot be outsourced.

"Your emotions can give you valuable information – about yourself, other people, and situations... The good news is that **emotional intelligence can be nurtured, developed, and augmented** – it isn't a trait that you either have or don't have."

—HENDRIE WEISINGER

(59)

Is **EQ** the worst-ever buzzword in the corporate world?

Probably (besides synergistically), but that doesn't mean it's not important.

Emotions are instant; they happen to us. Feelings are a choice; we choose them, and they are contagious.

Embrace all of your emotions. Then decide if they are real or helpful, and choose which ones to keep.

What we focus on expands.

Emotional Intelligence is understanding and managing your response to emotions so you can have better feelings and outcomes. EQ, as Dr. Daniel Goleman teaches consists of 4 main areas:
1. Self-Awareness
2. Self-management
3. Social-Awareness
4. Relationship-Management

Learn to master these four areas through daily practice and focus. Think about your thoughts and adjust to make your thoughts match your desired goals. Think about your actions and adjust to make your actions match your desired goals. The more you understand yourself and others and then take deliberate action, the more success in sales and in life you will find.

"The harder things get, the
better you get."

—SAM BRACKEN

60

Hustle much? Prove it.

Everyone thinks they work hard.

Working hard at the wrong things isn't really working hard. It might be difficult, it might be hard—but it is not work, work has a specific and defined purpose with a focused outcome.

Most don't. Everyone thinks they hustle; few do. Most people who actually work hard don't have time to let others know they work hard. If you want to work hard, do it; don't talk about it.

When it gets hard, the best sales reps work harder and they become better.

Those who work hardest and smartest get rewarded. True success means you do what you are committed to – through effort. So you work hard to keep your family commitments. So you work hard to keep your work commitments. So you work hard to keep your relationship, health, and mental commitments. That is what it means to hustle: to work hard to honor your commitments, whatever they may be.

"It usually takes me more
than three weeks to prepare a
good impromptu speech."

—MARK TWAIN

61

Practice & Prepare.

If you don't prepare well, it is 100% your fault. You can prepare. You need to prepare.

Why do some sales folks think they don't need to practice, that they can just wing it?

I never could. I practice all the time.

No professional ever enters the arena without practice. It doesn't matter their role or event.

A pianist playing at Carnegie Hall practices. A baseball player getting ready for opening day practices. Professional speakers who have given 1,000 speeches still practice.

Without practice, you are not a professional.

The more you practice, the more prepared you will be.

Do what the philosopher, clinical psychologist, and former Harvard professor, Jordan B. Peterson teaches: *"Work as hard as you possibly can at one thing and see what happens."*

Luck is created when hard work finds preparation and is introduced to opportunity.

"The most successful sellers,
are the ones who lead
masterful sales conversations
and **show up prepared**."

—MIKE SHULTZ

62

Prepare for every **sales** call (phone, video, in-person).

Create a "call plan."

On one piece of paper, be able to answer the following:
1. The customer's goals, guesstimated.
2. Your call objective. (Always start with the end in mind.)
3. Commercial insights to share.
4. Questions to ask (goals, discovery, needs, pain, impact of pain).
5. Anticipated challenges and concerns.
6. Biggest benefit and value to customers/users.
7. Urgency statement: Why you? Why now?
8. Desired next steps.

Do this for every call. No matter what. Just get it done.

"Learning fast is more
important than prestige."

—CHRISTOPHER ENGMAN

You probably don't need a mentor...

WRONG!

You do. Everyone does. Make mentorship a priority. Mentors help you learn, faster.

You need someone to guide you and support you. You need someone who has seen the road before to ask the difficult questions.

Like a picture to a word, a good mentor is worth more than 1,000 books.

Find someone who has done what you want to do and serve them. Once you have proven your value, ask them to mentor you.

Next, become a great student. Learn from your mentor. Prioritize the relationship. Spend time with your mentor, do what they say to do, and show gratitude. As Oprah says: *"Be thankful for what you have; you'll end up having more. If you concentrate on what you don't have, you will never, ever have enough."* Once you show your appreciation, go mentor others. We all know the best way to learn is to teach. (You need a coach too!)

"Process is important. Research is important. The pitch is important. But, the reality is I can learn more in 15 minutes asking the right questions, to the right person and listening, than most people can find out reading an entire company website."

—DERRIS MOORE

64

Show, Don't Tell.

Stop talking so much. Ask more questions.

Listen more. Once you have asked and listened, show. Instead of telling, just show them.

Show with real stories. Show with real examples. Show with real scenarios. When you tell, they might hear; when you show, they will see.

Because of their courage and empathy, the very best sales reps develop the skills they need to help make important connections with the right people. They connect by consulting (diagnosing) and then selling value. They usually do this through stories, memorable stories. The best sales reps use stories to demonstrate real (aligned) value while setting up unique positioning with relevant differentiators.

"Asking the right questions
and asking insightful
questions will give you a
better understanding about
who you are connecting
to and how you may be of
service."

—LORI RICHARDSON

65

If you can't **ask questions**, you can't sell.

Selling is not about YOU. It is especially not about YOUR PRODUCT.

So talk less. The best way to talk less is to ask great questions that inspire your future partner to talk. When the client wants to talk, they are showing that they trust you. The more thoughtful and more high-quality the question, the more likely they will trust you.

When you ask questions, do so from a place of pure curiosity. Once you know them, you can help them.

Also, ask them questions along the way. When travelling, you don't check the GPS just at the beginning; you are constantly checking the current position to make sure you are on the right track. In sales, you must do the same thing with questions.

"Discipline Equals Freedom."

—JOCKO WILLINK

66

Don't EVER, EVER **Overcome** Objections. (Sort of...)

Objections are not real. They are 100% created by perception.

Of course, you must get past no. You must get past the instant reflex of every buyer wanting to say no. Sales pros know it is about being patient and smart enough to understand the true motivations with a super strong desire to help and keep helping.

If you think you need to overcome objections, you are doing it wrong. Solve problems, create solutions, provide new opportunities, empower success. Whatever you do, don't overcome objections. You are on the same team; you should be on the same side. When you treat a no or a question or rejection as an objection, you know your mindset is not correct. In most sales scenarios, a no is just a chance to prove yourself and help them eventually get what they want anyway. (Only in sales – not in dating, marriage, personal, or family situations.)

Partnerships create the future together. If you are working toward partnership, objections don't exist and everything is turned into opportunity.

You can prevent objections though. You can block future objections by addressing them and solving them before they are realized. This way the road to the partnership starts off much more smoothly.

"Gratitude is the key to happiness. When gratitude is practiced regularly and from the heart, it leads to a richer, fuller and more complete life."

—VISHEN LAKHIANI

(67)

Be grateful. You will **thank me** later.

Showing gratitude is the number one way to increase happiness. Science says so.

When you are happy, you will perform better and more people will like you. Emotions are contagious. So if you are happy, you can help others be happy, too. When they are happy and they like you, it is easier to get aligned on goals and objectives.

1. Every morning write down five things you are grateful for.
2. Every afternoon call one person to tell them why you are thankful for them.
3. Every night write down all the good that happened that day.

If you do these three things every single day, you will become a much better version of yourself.

"Life happens at the level of events, not words."

—ALFRED ADLER

Create Impactful Scenarios

Scenarios are stories where you make the customer the hero. Scenarios build trust.

Scenarios are stories that the client connects with because the same situations are happening to them. Asking questions based on scenarios leads to better information. Once they have explained different situations, you can fill in the gaps with the best solution, or even better, create a new reality. When you are using scenarios to help them see a better future, be certain that the scenarios focus on where your product or service can have the most impact. Make sure your demos are scenario-based, rather than feature-based.

Scenario application is not just about making the current situation better. Most of the time, a good scenario paints a picture that was never thought of before or shows an insight that is only gained through serious expertise. In sales, the value you add is your ability to help people have hope for better experiences. Once they have hope, they can make decisions that drive growth and satisfaction. In order to help drive that hope, the future you help them paint needs to be clear and compelling.

The vision needs to become real to them, and that is done through the effective use of scenario-creation and explanation. Scenarios cannot be created, however, until true listening and deep understanding are already in place.

The best way to help others, especially in sales, is to be open, to be honest, and to stay curious.

If you do that, your scenarios will always make the most sense to your potential clients, and your business will grow.

"It's OK to have your eggs
in one basket as long as you
control what happens to that
basket."

—ELON MUSK

69

Commitment

The fastest way to achieve your dreams is to commit to them.

Once you are committed to something, nothing else will stand in your way. Commitment is more than a desire, a hope, or a dream. Commitment basically means other options don't exist. Commitment is a decision that is proven by action. Everything comes down to commitment. You will do (as you have always done) whatever you commit to.

"When you care about helping other people generate the results that they can't generate without you, your outward **focus** is part of what creates a preference and makes you easier to buy from."

—ANTHONY IANNARINO

70

Help your prospects commit, then they will make better buying decisions.

Commitment is shown in action. Help your prospects keep their commitments. That is how they will grow as well.

Anthony Iannarino teaches in his book, *The Lost Art of Closing*, that in order to sell effectively, you need to be able to help your prospects make and keep the following commitments:

The commitment to...
1. Spend the needed TIME.
2. EXPLORE the problem and solution.
3. Being open to CHANGE.
4. COLLABORATE with your team.
5. GAIN CONSENSUS.
6. INVEST resources.
7. REVIEW proposals by decision makers.
8. RESOLVE all concerns.
9. DECIDE to take a specific action.
10. Work together to EXECUTE a solution.

"Anyone can sell products by dropping their prices, but it does not breed loyalty."

—SIMON SINEK

71

Loyal fans are always on the same side.

Sales should not be adversarial. You are helping people get what they want. Learn to get on the same side of the table as your partner.

Most individuals will do just about anything for those who justify their failures, erase their fears, encourage their dreams, help them fight their battles, and support their beliefs.

If you can do all five, you can build loyal – to the end of the world and back – fans of you and your brand.

"Keep your sales pipeline full
by prospecting continuously."

—BRIAN TRACY

72

When everything is falling apart, **pick up the phone**.

When your pipeline isn't too healthy, *call someone.*

When your prospects have new roadblocks, *call someone.*

When your partners misunderstand everything, **call someone.**

The human voice is powerful. It can be calming. It is reassuring. Use your voice to grow your business and solve problems.

"Customers don't buy from
people they don't trust."

—GEOFFREY JAMES

73

In the end, hard work, true value, and relationships **always win**.

It is common sense.

If you get up every time you fail, if you help give people what they need and want, and if people trust you, then of course, they will do business with you.

"An abundance mentality leads to sustainable happiness and satisfaction in relationships. It eliminates contrived competition and brings people together to accomplish great things."

—BLAKE HANSEN

74

Build Consensus

There must be a need.

A need to improve, a problem that needs to be fixed, or a need for new opportunity growth. Help identify and evangelize that need and then provide solutions. Real sales professionals only sell to true needs. Once you have defined the need, you can begin to build consensus.

Often, you will need to sell into organizations that have multiple stakeholders.

Different stakeholders have different needs. Your conversations must be strategically based on the value each stakeholder needs to receive.

To build consensus, you must ask better questions. You need to know who is involved, who could be involved, and who will be impacted. Make sure everyone impacted by the decision is included and has given approval. This is where you tailor your value story to the needs and wants of each stakeholder.

"Production over perfection is
the key to success."

—BRANDON BORNANCIN

75

There is a magic potion.

Complaints are magic.

It means the customer wants you to solve them. It means there is still hope. It means they are telling you exactly what to fix! Search for complaints and use them to create better relationships and better outcomes. Whenever possible, listen to complaints face to face (video-call or in-person). Even if the customer tells you on the phone, get on a video conference or fly out that evening and in the morning let them tell you the complaint again. Promise to do whatever you can and go to work.

Complaints work like magic in strengthening relationships, if corrected properly.

"You need to give your customers fewer reasons to be disloyal, and the best way to make that happen is to reduce customer effort."

—MATT DIXON

76

People buy from whomever is **easiest** to buy from.

Can you answer these questions? (Easily?)

- Are you available?
- Do you make contracts simple?
- Is it easy to solve problems with you?
- Is it easy to share information?
- Do you respond?
- Do you share insights?
- Are you flexible in your sales process?

To truly make it easy, you need to be customer-focused, and you need to understand them, their needs, and their business environment. And more than just the knowledge, you have to care enough to change how you run your business so that the life of your customer is easier.

Making it easy is tangible. If you are focusing every action they take on "making it easy," the results will be a better experience for the client.

If you are reducing the effort your clients need to put forth to work with you, you will create true loyalty and increase sales.

Just make it easy to buy from you.

"We make a mess when we fail
to listen."

—DEB CALVERT

77

The best questions **get** the best **answers**.

Those who ask the best questions will always win. (It shows you care)

In every sales interaction make sure you ask the right types of questions. You CAN and should ask yes or no questions and open-ended questions. It doesn't matter if you know the answer or not. You are not trying to trick or manipulate. Ask questions to learn, to understand, and to get your partners to think in a new way.

In every meeting, the questions need to create and bring to light information that can help everyone. They need to be driven by curiosity. They should revolve around discovering the goals, needs, and wants of the client. They should be asked to understand the current or future pain and the impact of that pain.

Some of the best questions are:
- Can you tell me what... means?
- Maybe, tell me how...
- Please, explain... for me...
- Does... make sense?
- If you don't accomplish... what will that mean for your business?
- How does that impact...?

And after every answer, you can always ask:

"Can you tell me more about that?"

"Focus on a goal and mission that is bigger than yourself and then load tactics and action steps in front of you to keep you focused. When you do that, no matter what type of adversity comes your way, you will not be distracted and you will persevere!"

—HEATHER R. YOUNGER

Dreams define your ideal.
Goals define your actions.

Always take actions that align your goals and dreams together. Couple your action with belief and faith.

Russell M. Nelson, President of the Church of Jesus Christ of Latter-day Saints and pioneering surgeon for open-heart surgery said that: *"Truly, faith is the power that enables the unlikely to accomplish the impossible."*

Set goals that are specific and measurable. Keep a record of your accomplishments. Adjust as needed. When you fail, and you will fail as you grow – learn from every experience. Bill Eckstrom reminds you to: *"Know that setbacks can become stepping stones."* As you focus on your goals and take proper action, you can use every situation for your eventual advantage.

"No one can master sales. It's a philosophy. There is always more to learn."

—LEE SALZ

They are not coming.

If you think someone is going to save you...

If you think someone will rescue you...

Stop.

No one is coming.

Save yourself first.

No one else is coming.

You need to embrace every role and outperform expectations. Keep learning and keep serving. That is how you truly build a career that has meaning. It is found in your actions (not hopes or dreams). But hopefully you let your hopes and dreams guide your actions because, at the end, actions are what really matter.

"The truth is that everyone is afraid of rejection. Everyone. **You can** be the most confident person in the world, but in the back of your head the fear of rejection will never go away. The best salespeople look that fear in the eye, deal with it, and **overcome it every single day**."

—ROBERT KIYOSAKI

Everything you want in life is on the other side of the "**ASK**."

The first person to ask is yourself. That is how you will create the biggest change.

Know what you want. Know why you want it. The purpose is stronger than the object. Once you know both, you can begin to use specifics to ask better questions. The next step to ask those you know for help and for support. Stu Heinecke teaches that: *"To create explosive growth in the scale of your career or business, you need to know what to ask for."*

The better you get at asking the right people (yourself included) the right questions, the more success you will create. Those who care the most will ask the best questions.

"I had thought the destination was what was important, but it turned out it was the journey. In order to really find happiness, you need to continue looking for opportunities that you believe are meaningful, in which you will be able to learn new things, to succeed, and be given more and more responsibility to shoulder."

—CLAYTON M. CHRISTENSEN

(81)

When you really want something, keep asking until you **find a way** to make it happen.

Often you will have to change your approach, or change your message, but eventually if what you are doing has value, you will find an audience. Is your "why" big enough to pursue when faced with rejection and lack of support, even by your father (or best friend, or partner, or colleagues)? No matter what I have sold in the past, no matter the industry – whether it was durable goods, commodities, investments, or software – every business transaction and sale required me to gain a commitment from the client to change. Growth comes from change.

As Skip Prichard, the author of *The Book of Mistakes,* teaches: *"Our thoughts can empower or imprison. They empower when we try something new, and they imprison when we let them convince us to stay comfortable."*

Asking starts as a thought. Until you ask for the change, that change will never happen. Once you ask, you can get the commitment and provide the path forward. Commit to your growth and help your clients commit to theirs.

"There is no path – which means the field is wide open for exploration, and it's time to blaze your own trail."

—SARAH ELKINS

Little actions always combine to **create** massive **results**.

Those results – good or bad – are up to you and your daily actions, which are your habits.

Habits are things you repeatedly do, so while the situations change, your attitude, values, and character do not. These habits determine success.

Success comes from discipline:
- Make sure you are disciplined in doing everything you must do right now. (Duty)
- Make sure you are disciplined in always and only doing what is important. (Priorities)
- Make sure you are disciplined in doing all of the little things the right way. (Details)

Discipline comes from practice and caring enough to focus on the right things.

"I always tell my kids if you lay down, people will step over you. But if you keep scrambling, if you keep going, someone will always, always give you a hand. Always. But you gotta keep dancing, you gotta keep your feet moving."

—MORGAN FREEMAN

(83)

Nothing beats **action**. Nothing beats doing the **work**.

Growing up spending summers milking cows taught me one thing – cows usually won't milk themselves. Your clients aren't going to come running to you unless you first build a system and reason for them to do so.

While tools, software, systems, and processes might create shortcuts or needed hacks, they are not substitutes for effort and action. The only way to get work done is to do it. People respect effort and dedication and expertise.

You always find better results when you are willing to do more, learn more, and help more.

When being sold to now, I always notice those who go the extra mile. Working with clients and partners, you want to be with people who do the work and then do more. Make sure it is you that is getting noticed by your clients, and your sales will increase.

"The longer I work in this business, the more I realize how everything comes down to one thing – **belief**.

Belief creates the customer. Belief creates the results."

—RUSSELL BRUNSON

When you **sell** something, just go to where the people are, and give them **what they want**.

No matter how good your product or service is, you cannot sell it to clients who do not exist.

If you are not near them (physically or virtually), they do not exist and neither do you.

Specifically, you can only sell to those whom you spend time around. And once you spend enough time with them, you will know exactly what they want.

From experience selling complex solutions, I know that often customers don't know what they want. They don't know what they need. The role of a professional salesperson is to help them get to where they want to go, even if they do not know where that is at the start of the journey. Those who sell always find ways to help. Those who sell can develop ways to create value for others.

"**Not finance.**
Not strategy.
Not technology.

It is **teamwork** that remains
the ultimate competitive
advantage, both because it **is**
so powerful and so rare."

—PATRICK LENCIONI

(85)

Teams **win**. Sell as a team.

Use all of your resources.

Team-selling requires careful orchestration. Make sure everyone that is involved knows the overall objective and plan. Teams are powerful because they are diverse sets of people with diverse experiences working together to solve the same problem. Diversity in thought creates creative solutions and better outcomes.

"The best coaching questions are ones you don't know the answer to. If you already know the answer, then you're closing, not coaching."

—KEITH ROSEN

(86)

The **Transition** from Star Performer **to** Sales **Leader**
(VP, Manager, Director)

Sales leadership requires specific skills and performance. As a sales leader, you need to know what to do and how to do it.

You need to:

1.   Train, monitor, and coach your team.

2.   Create and execute strategy. Tactics are tactics. Strategy is strategy. Tactics are not a strategy. A real strategy is when the tactics are chosen, organized, planned, and resourced. Multiple tactics working together for a certain goal and aligned with purpose, support, and thoughtfulness is how basic actions turn into a true strategy.

3.   Perform executive, cross-functional collaboration.

4.   Help your team sell to the C-suite and close the largest deals.

And the most important is...? Not training, not mentoring, but...
Coaching.

To be a great sales leader, learn to coach. Coaching is much more than training and mentoring. Coaching is the single best way to get high performance from an individual and team. Coaches are personally invested; they see the big picture, they want to teach, and they know how to ask all the right questions that drive performance. Great sales leaders are great coaches who encourage greatness.

"Prayer works. Prayer changes things. Perhaps more important, prayer changes you. **Prayer changes your brain**."

—CRAIG GROESCHEL

Want something?
Ask for it.

What is the best way to get what you want? Ask for it.

And if you want to get better – at anything – ask yourself to be better. Here are some great ways to do just that. Ask God, and ask yourself:

1. **"Do I show enough gratitude?"**
    Gratitude is the key to unlocking happiness. Happiness helps drive performance, fulfillment, and success. Are you writing down ten things you are grateful for every day? Do you show people how much you care?

2. **"What does my 'gut' tell me?"**
    You know that gut feeling you have? Trust it. Trust your intuition. Then question the reason you have that gut feeling. You will learn tons about yourself. You have had immense experiences, and your subconscious processes them all.

    Your "gut" is a driving force curating your emotions, knowledge, and experiences. Use it and learn from it.

3. **"Why do I do what I do?"**

REALLY CARE FOR THEM

Why are you doing what you are doing right now? What makes you want to do it? How does what you are doing help you realize your ultimate goals? Do your actions help others? What can you learn?

Focus on learning. Focus on experiences. The more experiences you have to learn from, the stronger your ability to help others becomes.

4. **"Is this the best I can do?"**
   Ask yourself:
   Am I doing my best? Can I do more?

   If you can't do more, awesome; just keep going. If you can... get better. Do more. Try harder. Work smarter. Ask others to help you do better.

   Master your skill. Master your craft.

5. **"Am I using my mentor or coach effectively?"**
   Mentors and coaches are not always the same person, even though they can be. You might need both, but always have at least one.

   Help them help you by actually listening and applying what they teach you. Ask them deeper questions. Ask them to help you stretch yourself. Ask them, "Why?"

6. **"Do I love myself?"**
   This question is hard to answer. Answer it anyway.
   Check your self-talk. Am I negative about my actions or thoughts? Do I give others more credit than I give myself? Do I treat my mental and physical self with respect? Am I truly loving myself?

   When you love yourself, you can better love other people.

7.   **"Am I helping enough people?"**
     At the end of our lives, our relationships are the only things that
     matter. The people whom we have helped, and who have helped us,
     build our lives. The more we help others, the more fulfillment and
     satisfaction we will feel.

While success as a destination is hard to find, success as a journey can be
experienced every day.

Help more. Make your journey better and bring others with you.

"**Life is truly** lived through moments of **service** to our fellow human beings."

—LARRY LEVINE

(88)

Greatness requires **consistency**.

You are not great until you do great things over and over again.

You are not great until you are consistent.

Lasting greatness is measured by how well you consistently serve and uplift others.

"Use boldness, but not
overbearance; and also
see that ye bridle all your
passions, that ye may be filled
with love; see that ye refrain
from idleness."

—ALMA THE PROPHET, TO HIS SON SHIBLON

89

Be Bold + Work Hard + Stop Caring What Others Think.

Peace comes when you stop caring about what others think and what you might be missing out on.

You need to care, but only about the right things. You can only live one life: yours. You cannot live anyone else's life. Do not worry about what others are doing, and especially do not worry about what they think about you. Let go of your outward identity and only focus on what truly matters – relationships and service. That is where you will find peace and ultimate success.

A simple formula for gaining success in sales while still feeling at peace without stress:

Be bold. Care about the outcomes of others that you can help with. Stay in control. Love others. Work hard.

"It is not your title that makes you a leader. It is your influence, inspiration and initiative."

—OLEG VISHNEPOLSKY

90

Sales professionals **lead**.

Sales is leadership.

Leadership is sales.

All true leaders are also sales experts.

All sales professionals need to always be leading.
*   Lead yourself first.
*   Lead your colleagues.
*   Lead your customers.
*   Lead with vision, integrity, and energy, and you will create true loyalty.

Leading others takes effort. Leading others takes care. Author and leadership expert Gifford Thomas teaches us that: *"Leadership is about people, it's about inspiring people to believe that the impossible is possible, it is about developing and building people to perform at heights they never imagine, and it's about making a positive impact on your community, your company, your department, your employees, and by extension the world."*

The more care is shown through concern, curiosity, accountability, and vision – the more leadership loyalty is built, trust is created, and positive results produced.

"Simplicity is complex. It's never simple to keep things simple. Simple solutions require the most advanced thinking."

—RICHIE NORTON

91

Simplicity is one of your best friends.

Anytime you can take something extremely complex, and make it simple, you will create true value.

And value, when understood, always creates strong relationships and new clients. Making things simple is always the right move.

Brigette Hyacinth believes that: *"Keeping things simple means keeping them effective and efficient. Being able to share complex things in a simple way requires maturity, wisdom and a clear understanding of the situation."*

When you make it simple for your client, it shows you care.

"If you want to become
invaluable in a workplace – in
any community – just do the
things no one else is doing.
Difficult is necessary."

—JORDAN B. PETERSON

92

You need a creed.

This is my Personal Sales Creed:
(You can steal this one, or make your own.)
- I care about others.
- I am the master of my craft. I am a professional.
- I am constantly learning, training, and developing all of my skills.
- I place the customer above all else.
- I plan and am always prepared.
- I believe trust wins.
- I am honest.
- I am curious.
- I am dedicated.
- I am passionate.
- I love helping people.
- I listen more than I talk.
- I teach, explain, simplify, and create value for everyone with every conversation.
- I am positive because I know that what I focus on expands.
- I am resilient.
- I am grateful.
- Everyone feeds off of my enthusiasm and energy.

Read your creed daily. Say it out loud, think about it, believe it, live it – sign your name to it.

"Talk less and sell more."

—COLLEEN STANLEY

93

3 Things to **Always Remember**

Always remember that...

1. It is not about you, your feelings, or your products. If you stay customer-focused, you have a much better chance at success.

2. If you can find enough people to help, you will sell forever. It is 100% up to you.

3. You choose your thoughts, your thoughts determine your actions, and your actions determine your life. Choose wisely.

If you actually care, you will do what it takes to be the best. For yourself, for your team, and for your clients. When you are willing to help, to serve, to care – your customers are willing to buy.

"I have come to the
frightening conclusion that
I am the decisive element.
It is my personal approach
that creates the climate.
It is my daily mood that
makes the weather. I possess
tremendous power to make
life miserable or joyous. I
can be a tool of torture or an
instrument if inspiration; I
can humiliate or humor, hurt
or heal. In all situations, it
is my response that decides
whether a crisis is escalated
or de-escalated, and a person
humanized or de-humanized.
If we treat people as they are,
we make them worse. If we
treat people as they ought
to be, we help them become
what they are capable of
becoming."

—GOETHE

(94)

Seeing people as people will **create unimaginable growth**.

Caring for others is how you will unlock your potential.

True growth only happens when you begin to see other people as people and not as objects.

People can change and are of infinite worth. Objects require you to change them. Once you begin to see others the right way, you will stop blaming, and start to grow.

And best of all, you will treat yourself the right way as well. You will begin to show how much you care, and then your entire world will change. Those who care the most, will always find a way to succeed. All you need to do is to **really care for them**.

"We have to get out of our
comfort zone if we're going
to grow. And that's the
key point. Necessity is the
crucible of learning."

—JAMES MUIR

Show You Care By Learning & Doing.

When you care, it shows.

Some people sacrifice everything. They are the ones you can count on.
Some people do whatever it takes. They are the ones you can trust.
Some people care enough to be present. They are the ones you honor.

The more you care, the more you will sacrifice.
The more you care, the more you do what it takes.
The more you care, the more present you will be.

When you care, you learn.
Once you know, you can do.
Once you learn and know, you can show you care.

"Leadership is about love. You love others by desiring to help them and you love yourself by believing that you can."

—JOSH WEEKS

(96)

Sales Is Leadership

The best leaders I ever had, cared.
The best leaders I ever had, sold me.
They showed up, they were present.

I trusted their intention. I trusted their motivation. I trusted that they cared. I was sold on who they were and what they stood for.

The people who lead the best, care the most.
The people who lead the best, sell the most as well.

They sell ideas and vision, they sell confidence and courage, they sell trust and respect.

Yet, selling is much more than leadership and management. Selling affects every aspect of every business and role.

If you want a better job – care more so you can sell better.
If you want to make more money – care more so you can sell better.
If you want to be a better leader – care more so you can sell better.
As we learn to sell, we learn to lead.

Those who care the most sell and lead the best.
The more leaders we have, the higher we all will rise.

"Apathy is the enemy."

—BO MOLOCZNIK

Take Courage

Courage defeats apathy. Apathy is the opposite of caring. When you care, you build courage and overcome apathy.

Courage is the ultimate secret tool for developing confidence and self-esteem. The theories are easy, the action is hard.

Courage is the willingness and ability to take proper action in the face of fear, grief, or pain.

Courage isn't just for a few, the rich, the outgoing, the brave, or talented. Everyone can develop courage.

Courage is what we all need. It is what people are attracted to. Leadership expert and author John Eades teaches: *"People don't follow titles; they follow courage."*

Courage is created. You can instantly create small moments of courage that constantly and consistently build over time. Each moment of courage helps create the new you. True courage allows you to maximize your potential. It allows you to become the best version of yourself. Do what is right no matter the emotional obstacle and you will gain tremendous courage. Courage is easier when you care enough.

"You don't have to be the
victim of your environment.
You can also be the architect
of it."

—JAMES CLEAR

(98)

Senior Executives Only Care About 4 Things.

Top leadership gets paid to make the hard decisions. To sell to them, you must convince them to convince themselves that your solution will give them the outcomes they crave. This is what they want and need; this is what they care about:

1. Reducing Risk (Lower Risk)
2. Increasing Revenue (Grow Revenue)
3. Reducing Cost (Lower Cost)
4. Increasing Market Share (Grow Market Share)

But, it needs to be specific; what you say needs to connect emotionally first and be relevant to their understanding and situation. Tell them future stories around those 4 areas, and you will sell well. If you care enough to sell them what they want and need, you will always find sales success. When you sell well, you are creating a new reality for those you serve. When you care about others, when you care about the results, and your actions match your desires, then you are not a victim anymore.

"What we love determines
what we seek."

—DIETER F. UCHTDORF

21 Rules For Success

Here is what the "real-world" taught me:

1. Helping others achieve their dreams is the best way to achieve yours.
2. Your best investment will always be to take care of those you trust and love.
3. Nothing is more important than courage. Courage is taking the proper action in the face of fear, grief, or pain.
4. Never finish tomorrow what you can do today, especially in sales and business. (All business is sales.)
5. The best leaders are always learning and adapting. They create themselves step-by-step, day-by-day, so that every year they are a new, better version of themselves.
6. Having a purpose greater than yourself enables you to overcome any setback.
7. Ask for advice from those you want to become like.
8. Solve other people's problems, so they have a reason to trust and like you.
9. Understanding the entire ecosystem and each moving part is key to vision and good decision making.
10. Sales is about caring so much that you are persistent enough to eventually help.
11. Learn from mistakes.
12. The best way to lead is by example. The second best way is through encouragement.

13. Never let others pressure you to make a decision. Make every decision on your own timetable or not at all.
14. Teams can solve problems better than individuals.
15. Learn as much as you can as fast as you can. Make career decisions that allow you to learn and do.
16. Be true at all times. Integrity eventually always matters.
17. Analyze with your mind but trust your gut.
18. Confidence is key to relationships and good decision making. Confidence is not pride. Confidence is knowing who you are and what you stand for no matter what others do or say.
19. Your true principles and values must never change even if your plan, path, or method do.
20. The greatest moments of success are often small, seemingly inconsequential choices. Be prepared and stay focused to make the right choice at the right time since you never know which choice will be the one that changes your life.
21. If you are surrounded by people better than you, you will become better and so will your organization. Focus on surrounding yourself with great talent, integrity, work ethic, and common sense.

"The world makes room for passionate people. You need desire to be fully alive and you need vision to fulfill your desires. You become what you envision yourself being. Greatness is the result of visionaries who persevere, focus, believe, and prepare. It is a habit, not a birthright."

—LEWIS HOWES

CONCLUSION

Caring creates passion. Passion produces results. Thinking about others and what they need and want and feel is the secret to opening doors for you and for them. The more you care, the more you will achieve. Caring is proven with action.

As you learn to care more, your sales will increase.
As you learn to care more, your relationships will improve.
As you learn to care more, you will find your passion and live your purpose.

Learning is good. Taking action is better. Caring for others along the way is best.

Keep going. Keep doing. You are needed. You are stronger than you think.

ACKNOWLEDGMENTS

A special thank-you to my wonderful mother, Birgit McCracken – who courageously raised the 6 of us the right way, with love, and absent of complaint.

Without the guidance and sacrifice of my older brother, Geromy McCracken, none of this would have happened. You are needed and appreciated.

Thanks a million, to Terry Whalin, David Hancock and the Morgan James team for exercising the courage to publish this book.

A very heartfelt thank-you to everyone who supported me in my journey so far. Your example and counsel are remembered and appreciated. An apology in advance to anyone missed, but here is a list to just name a few:

Ada Hinton - Alessandra Dorr Darze – Amelia Ong - Amy Blaschka - Andrew Wan - Andria Finau - Annamaria Weaver - Anthony Castro - Anthony Iannarino - Benjamin Unfried - Benjamin Wallace - Bert Burraston - Björn Hansen-Sackey - Blaine Bergeson - Blake Watterson - Bo Molocznik - Boyce Weber - Boyd Hoffman - Brian Pickup - Brigham Johnson - Brock Smith - Cade Bryant - Cameron Curtis - Carlos Santos - Christina Ashworth - Christopher Engman - Cobi McCracken – Connie Hawkins - Craig Forbush - Dan Mower - Daryl Beeson - David Chang - David Keele - David Lindsay - Dennis Grimmer - Derek Walls - Derris Moore - Donald Hinton - Doug Andersen - Drew McDonald - Elias Delgado - Eric Huppi - Eva Katarina McCracken - Gayle Weber - Göran Hansen-Sackey - Heather Younger - Jacob Beutler - Jacob McCracken - Jake Ellison – Janet Andersen - Jannika Hansen-Sackey - Jared Cannon - Jared Ong - Jason Hoopes - Jason Porter - Jason Weaver - Jeb Blount - Jeff Haden - Jeremy Hansen - Jesse Fox - Jessica Lines Hansen - Jim Ferrell - Joe Belliston - Jon Millar - Jon Sorenson - Jonathan Bench - Joseph Flinders - Josh Perez - Josh Weeks - Joshua Molina - Julia McCracken - Justin Hannig - Karen Abbott - Keeta McCracken - Kenneth Nyman - Kimberly Davis - Lamar Mays - Laura-Kay Mower - LeRyan Lambert - Levy Minharo - Lucia Dorr - Lucia McCracken - Marcello Mancini - Marcus McCoy - Maria Grimmer - Mark Hunter - Martin McCracken - Matt Adsero - Maupi Dorr - Maybelline McCoy - Micah Smith - Michael Holden - Michael Judd - Mike Bride - Mike Jones - Mike Meinzer - Mike Weber - Mike Weinberg - Mitch Kirkham - Mrs. Burkheimer - Nathan Bowlby - Nickolas Crawford - Nicolas Orrego - Pete Weber - Peter Alexander - Peter Ashworth - Piet Dorr - Preben Hansen-Sackey - Rob Englehorn - Ross Weber - Ryan Smith - Sam Bracken - Sarah Elkins - Scott Amoye - Scott Omae - Seth Ure - Seth Weber - Shane Ownbey - Solomon Sogunro - Sören Hansen-Sackey - Steve Holden - Steve McCracken - Susan Rooks - Suzi Ogden - Svenja Hansen-Sackey - Ted Ong - Tobias Hansen-Sackey - Tyson Weber - Vern Porter - Victor Antonio - Wes Wixom - Willy Rudé

ABOUT THE AUTHOR

Mareo McCracken is the Chief Revenue Officer at Movemedical, where he guides the sales, marketing, and customer success efforts. Prior to helping lead this Med Tech SaaS company, Mareo was the top performing salesperson at multiple companies in various industries including financial services, marketing, logistics, manufacturing, and commodities. Mareo's formal education includes a bachelor's degree in sociology from Brigham Young University and a master's degree in global leadership from the University of San Diego. Outside of family, reading, food, travel, church service and sports—driving organizational and individual growth are his passions. He loves finding and sharing meaning at the intersection of revenue, organizational health, and individual performance. Originally from Boise, Idaho, — and having lived, served, sold, and managed teams in London, Hong Kong, Yuma, San Diego, New York, Scottsdale, Houston, and Provo, — Mareo, his wife Emilie, and four children split their time between Salvador, Bahia, Brazil, and Boise, Idaho, USA.

CONTACT (Advisory + Consulting + Speaking)

For sales strategy support or execution on the ideas found is this book, reach out on LinkedIn:

https://www.linkedin.com/in/mareomccracken/

For inspiration, ideas, and insights:
www.mareomccracken.com

For the free downloadable guide that accompanies this book:
www.reallycareforthem.com

A free ebook edition is available with the purchase of this book.

To claim your free ebook edition:

1. Visit MorganJamesBOGO.com
2. Sign your name CLEARLY in the space
3. Complete the form and submit a photo of the entire copyright page
4. You or your friend can download the ebook to your preferred device

Print & Digital Together Forever.

Snap a photo   Free ebook   Read anywhere